A onetime lawyer with a love for language and justice, Abdu Murray shows how "we have mistaken autonomy for freedom" and how this "quest for autonomy has led us down an endless road with no traffic lights or painted lines." Aligning our hopes and desires with the truth can be costly but also freeing—as Abdu's own story reveals and Jesus poignantly declared. I've had the privilege of speaking and answering questions with Abdu in numerous university open forums. I've witnessed his keen mind, winsome humor, and sensitive spirit touch even the most ardent skeptic or follower of another faith, who have then engaged in conversation with him long after an event. This book is genuinely a breath of fresh air and an invaluable and accessible resource.

RAVI ZACHARIAS, author and speaker

In a world of moral confusion and situational ethics, my friend Abdu Murray brings masterful clarity and penetrating insights in his invaluable new book. This is a book you'll be telling all of your friends about!

LEE STROBEL, *New York Times* best-selling author; professor, Houston Baptist University

Abdu Murray's *Saving Truth* is powerfully poignant in an age in which internet fabrications "travel halfway around the world before truth has had a chance to put its boots on." There is no greater need in our post-truth "Culture of Confusion" than clarity respecting truth—what it is, how one can know it, and most importantly why we must submit our personal preferences to it, no matter the cost.

HANK HANEGRAAFF, president, the Christian Research Institute; host, *Bible Answer Man* broadcast and *Hank Unplugged* podcast; author of more than twenty books, including *MUSLIM: What You Need to Know about the World's Fastest-Growing Religion*

Saving Truth is a timely and important book. Murray deconstructs many of the confusions inherent in our "post-truth" culture. And yet he offers positive steps forward. I wish every Christian—and especially every Christian student—would read, study, and discuss this book.

SEAN MCDOWELL, Ph.D., professor, Biola University; internationally recognized speaker; author or coauthor of more than eighteen books including *Evidence That Demands a Verdict*

Everything we believe about culture, politics, or religion is shaped by our view of the world. Every Christian believer must, therefore, ask an important question: Are we allowing our Christian worldview to help us see reality clearly? In *Saving Truth*, Abdu Murray uses his considerable skills as a lawyer and Christian thinker to examine the most pressing issues of culture. His style is accessible and winsome, his message is relevant and timely. If you want some help evaluating the challenges facing our nation and Church, get this book.

> **J. WARNER WALLACE**—Cold-Case Detective; Senior Fellow, the Colson Center for Christian Worldview; Adjunct Professor of Apologetics, Biola University; author, *Cold-Case Christianity, God's Crime Scene*, and *Forensic Faith*

Whether we know it or not, the most important subject in the universe is Truth. Live by it and your eternity is secure. Ignore it and disaster awaits you in this life and forever. With this insightful book, my brilliant friend Abdu Murray is Saving Truth on the most relevant issues in our lives. Abdu brings you light and clarity to this increasingly dark and confusing world.

> **FRANK TUREK**, CrossExamined.org and coauthor, *I Don't Have Enough Faith to be an Atheist*

We seem to live in a world where we've moved on from the concept of truth, and yet we cannot ultimately live without it. Abdu Murray has a big brain and a big heart and provides a uniquely reliable, understanding, and hope-filled guide to the issues facing (and overwhelming) us today.

> **SAM ALLBERRY**, apologist with RZIM; author, *Is God Anti-Gay?*

SAVING
TRUTH

SAVING TRUTH

Finding Meaning & Clarity in a Post-Truth World

ABDU MURRAY

ZONDERVAN®

ZONDERVAN

Saving Truth
Copyright © 2018 by Abdu H. Murray

This title is also available as a Zondervan ebook.

This title is also available as a Zondervan audio book.

Requests for information should be addressed to:
Zondervan, 3900 *Sparks Dr. SE, Grand Rapids, Michigan 49546*

ISBN 978-0-310-56204-7 (hardcover)

ISBN 978-0-310-59983-8 (international trade paper edition)

Published in association with Andrew Wolgemuth and the literary agency of Wolgemuth & Associates, Inc.

Art direction: Tammy Johnson
Interior design: Denise Froehlich

Printed in the United States of America

18 19 20 21 22 23 /DHV/ 19 18 17 16 15 14 13 12 11 10 9 8 7 6 5 4 3 2 1

CONTENTS

1. The Blossoming of the Culture of Confusion. 11

2. Confusion and the Church:
   Seductions of a Post-Truth Mindset 27

3. Confusion's Consequences—
   Getting Freedom Wrong. 47

4. Clarity about Freedom 71

5. Clarity about Human Dignity. 93

6. Clarity about Sexuality, Gender, and Identity. 117

7. Clarity about Science and Faith 161

8. Clarity about Religious Pluralism 187

9. The Son through Fog: Clarity's Hope. 213

Acknowledgments. 227
Notes 229

*For Nicole, who like a Lake Michigan sunset, is a
"sea of glass mingled with fire." I hear your voice
whenever I put pen to paper. Your tenderness
for others and fiery faith inspire me always.*

CHAPTER 1

The Blossoming of the Culture of Confusion

You've been at an intersection before, waiting for the red light to change, and had that uneasy feeling: *Is the bus next to me moving forward or am I in reverse?*

The first thing you do to regain clarity and overcome the quick flash of vertigo is look at something that doesn't move—a mailbox, or the streetlight perhaps. Getting a fixed point of reference clears up your confusion and relieves the vertigo.

But what if there are no fixed points of reference? What then?

Some time ago I rode a car ferry across a river between Michigan and Ontario, Canada. One would think that a boat ferrying cars from one country to another would be large, holding many cars. Being from the Great Lakes state, I've ridden such grand ferries. This wasn't one of them. This ferry could hold two cars at most, and that morning it was just me. Because the ferry was so small and the trip so short, the deckhand asked me to stay in my car, which I happily did, given the young day's heat and my car's air-conditioning. Glancing down at my GPS just when the ferry pulled away from the dock, I didn't see us leave. Due to my car's mass and suspension, I didn't feel the boat gently pull away either. When I looked up and my eyes met the flowing river, my body told me I was stationary, but my eyes told me that we were moving. Looking at the ferry couldn't help me overcome the vertigo because it was moving too. And the ever-moving river didn't provide a fixed point of reference. There were no mailboxes or stoplights; a sure foundation was hard to find. So my dizziness persisted longer than it would have in a typical bus-at-the-intersection incident. Only the unmoving land across the river could abate my nausea and clear up my confusion.

Whenever we find ourselves in such situations, we instinctively try to end the disorientation by hurriedly locating a fixed point of reference that doesn't depend on our feelings. In fact, we recognize in those moments that our feelings are part of the problem. Imagine if in my situation the land itself was moving. Awash in the river, I wouldn't have been able to find a bearing. My feelings would have been unreliable. My confusion would have persisted and my uneasiness wouldn't have diminished.

Culturally speaking, in the past decade we have found ourselves adrift in a river with no bearings in sight. The cultural river we find ourselves in isn't narrow. We can barely see the land's outline. In fact, we departed from it so long ago that we've forgotten what solid earth feels like and have begun to question whether the land itself is anchored or afloat.

As if to put an exclamation mark on this situation, the Oxford Dictionaries selected "post-truth" as 2016's Word of the Year. The Oxford Dictionaries annually select a word that captures the culture's current mood and preoccupations. And post-truth does exactly that. According to Oxford Dictionaries, post-truth means "relating to or denoting circumstances in which objective facts are less influential in shaping public opinion than appeals to emotion and personal belief." Although the word dates back at least to 1992, the usage of post-truth ballooned in 2016 by 2,000 percent. That may seem shockingly high, but pause to reflect on the year. The American presidential election was marked by so many competing and false claims, allegations of fraud, and proven mistruths, it was difficult to know who to believe. Voices across the political spectrum were quick to condemn the other side with little or no facts and quick to defend their champion regardless of facts. Raw emotion dominated the megaphones of 2016's various protests such that the truth behind the controversies was drowned out. "Fake news" allowed agendas to advance regardless of, and often contrary to, the truth. Was it not the case that facts were dismissed as getting in the way of agendas? Was it not true that sensitivities to personal preferences and hair-trigger senses of outrage shaped debates and even determined the words considered acceptable in our supposedly free society? It's hard to think of a word better suited to the spirit of our age than "post-truth."

When the Soft Soil Is Harder

Post-truth has two modes. The first is a "soft" mode, by which I mean that we may acknowledge that truth exists—or that certain things are true—but we don't care about the truth if it gets in the way of our personal preferences.[1] In this soft mode of post-truth, the truth exists objectively, but our subjective feelings and opinions matter more. The second mode is "hard," by which I mean a willingness to propagate blatant falsehoods, knowing they're false, because doing so serves a higher political or social agenda.

The differences between the soft and hard modes of post-truth may be subtle, but they are significant. Both are troubling and both appear to be growing more pervasive. But I suspect the soft mode of post-truth is more dangerous. Allow me to explain.

Postmodernism emerged in the 1970s as a rejection of the notion of objective truth. (Postmodernism had other aims, but this was a defining goal.) "What's true for you may not be true for me," we would hear. Or someone might say, "There's no such thing as objective truth." Both statements are self-defeating and unlivable. Any denial of objective truth must itself be objectively true if it's to be meaningful. Yet despite its incoherence, postmodernism was quite resilient and remained influential in the West for decades.

Its luster has finally dulled. To be sure, in the past few years postmodernism has continued to pop up in culture. But like a mustard burp, its tang is now momentary and passing.[2] Where postmodernism failed because it was inherently incoherent, the post-truth mindset may succeed because it is not. It faces the problem of truth head-on. Unlike postmodernism, the post-truth mindset acknowledges objective truth, but subordinates it to preferences. That's dangerous, as logic and evidence don't have the same influence over the post-truth mindset that they had over a postmodern. In a post-truth age, if the evidence fits our preferences and opinions, then all is well and good. If it doesn't, then the evidence is deemed inadmissible or offensive, with offense being a kind of solvent against otherwise sound arguments. To mix metaphors a bit, the post-truth mindset is like bacteria that have mutated to become immune to antibiotics. Where truth and logic could combat postmodern bacteria, they seem powerless to arrest post-truth's infectiousness.

There Is No One Immune— No, Not One

Mixed reactions followed Oxford's announcement of post-truth as its 2016 Word of the Year. Some want to confine the post-truth mindset to politics, arguing that it occurred mainly within the context of the 2016 American presidential race and infected only one side, generally the side opposite one's own. Others instinctively claim post-truth as a positive development, the means to forge one's own destiny free of the shackles of tradition, facts, and even logic.[3]

Still others bemoan the post-truth mindset. Consider Kathleen Higgins' lament in her *Nature* article "Post-Truth: A Guide for the Perplexed." Shaken by the development of the post-truth mindset, she points out it may undermine scientific endeavor. "Science's quest for knowledge about reality presupposes the importance of truth, both as an end in itself and as a means of resolving problems. How could truth become passé?"[4]

Fascinatingly, she seems concerned only about how post-truth has become the traffic cop at the intersection of science and politics, particularly on the climate change issue. Higgins writes:

> Scientists and philosophers should be shocked by the idea of post-truth, and they should speak up when scientific findings are ignored by those in power or treated as mere

matters of faith. Scientists must keep reminding society of the importance of the social mission of science—to provide the best information possible as the basis for public policy. And they should publicly affirm the intellectual virtues that they so effectively model: critical thinking, sustained inquiry and revision of beliefs on the basis of evidence. Another line from Nietzsche is especially pertinent now: "Three cheers for physics!—and even more for the motive that spurs us toward physics—our honesty!"[5]

Isn't it interesting that Higgins seems to lay the problems of post-truth at the feet of others, while implying that scientists are immune from its influence?

My point is not to denigrate scientists or science. Some of my close friends are scientists of high integrity. Nor am I making a statement about climate change. Clearly, science has benefited all our lives, and I'm convinced science is a gift from God. My point is the post-truth virus is so powerful that it can infect all of us: politicians and voters, pastors and philosophers, soccer moms and baseball dads, and yes, even scientists.

One would think a writer for *Nature* would recognize that scientists—who many seem to think lose their susceptibility to human bias when they don a lab coat—are not immune from post-truth's infection. There is ample evidence that scientists are all too human. In January 2016, just as the post-truth year began, Adam Hoffman reported the surprising results of several studies that concluded the findings of certain sciences are difficult to reproduce.[6] One study asserted the findings in fewer than half of the psychology studies printed in prestigious journals could be reproduced.[7] Stanford University's John Ioannidis went so far as to say that across many scientific disciplines, "It can be proven that most claimed research findings are false."[8] Putting an alarming number to the problem, Ioannidis says, "We are getting millions of papers that go nowhere."[9]

In the face of such conclusions, Hoffman asks, "So why is this crisis in transparency and reproducibility happening in the first place?" His conclusion is telling. In addition to conscious or unconscious biases, scientists are under pressure to obtain "breakthrough results," and those are more likely to get published.[10] In other words, the hard work of honest and forthright research is being undermined by the academic definition of success. No area is immune to post-truth infection.

The irony ought to leap out at us. Higgins is perplexed by the rise of post-truth in politics, fearing it may undermine society's trust in scientists who "so effectively model" the intellectual virtues of "critical thinking, sustained inquiry and revision of beliefs on the basis of evidence." Yet she herself seems to succumb to post-truth, as she vaunts the virtues of scientists while ignoring the questionable conclusions of many scientific studies. In making a case that scientists are above being post-truth, she inadvertently demonstrates the opposite by letting her feelings about scientists overpower the facts.

The creep of post-truth is seen in how we gather information about the world to conform to what we *want* to be true, not to what actually *is* true. Stephen Marche makes this point in a biased, yet incisive, op-ed piece in the *Los Angeles Times*.[11] He notes that many of us get our news not from time-tested news sources, but from comedy and satire shows like *The Daily Show*, *Last Week Tonight*, and *Full Frontal with Samantha Bee*. These shows use comedians as faux journalists who mix facts with satire and mockery. The jokes have an obvious slant and are meant to make a point about a particular situation, rather than just report facts. All of that is fine in itself. I'm personally a fan of well-done satire. But what can happen is viewers lose perspective, with the encouragement of these shows' producers. Viewers watch, satisfied by the parody of "the other side" of an issue, while fooling themselves into thinking they are being informed. According to Marche, these shows are why "the Left has a post-truth problem, too." With so much satire masquerading as journalism, Marche bemoans that "post-fact life is funny but not ha-ha funny. Everything has become a joke and so nothing is anymore."[12]

Such shows are emblematic of post-truth's effect on culture. We don't look to facts to find out the truth. We look at editorialized facts to support our preferences. Post-truth isn't just a political issue either. It also infects our spiritual lives and influences how we seek answers to life's biggest questions.

A conversation I had with a young man a few years ago during a multiday speaking trip comes to mind. His parents approached me after one of my talks to tell me that their son was increasingly hardened to the gospel and would become combative during spiritual conversations. But he was interested in meeting with me nonetheless. So the following night after speaking, I sat down with him in the now-empty auditorium. I asked him about his biggest objections to Christianity, and he told me that the Bible was full of scientifically impossible fables and morally questionable stories. As I began to address his objections, I was fascinated by his willingness to listen. This was surprising, given his parents' description of him. Our interchange was going so well, I thought I'd simply ask where he'd gotten his arguments against Christianity.

"I watch a lot of YouTube videos by atheists," he responded. "I hear these things on *The Daily Show* on Comedy Central. And I read a lot of posts on the Internet." As it turned out, he hadn't read a single book or scholarly article nor taken the time to ask a pastor or theologian a single question.

"Those are really your sources for your worldview?" I asked. "Have you ever read a book by a real scholar or watched videos by credible Christians responding to the things you've watched?" His answer was simply "No." It had never occurred to him to do so. He bypassed sincere inquiry so he could marshal the "facts" he was interested in and hear arguments he was predisposed to agree with. He wanted to disbelieve, so he turned to sources that would reinforce his preferences. This is a quite human tendency, innate in all of us. It's called "confirmation bias." Truth didn't matter. His preferences mattered. But—and I do believe this is God's grace—by the time we were finished talking, truth had started to matter to him, and he was asking me for additional sources to read.

The Post-Truth Seed in the Garden's Soft Soil

As startling as recent developments have been, we should remember that the practice of subordinating truth to feelings is ancient. Biblically speaking, the post-truth mindset flowering today originally germinated in a lush garden long ago. God gave Adam and Eve freedom in Eden so that they could enjoy relationship with Him—the very reason for which they were created. They had but one restriction: they could not eat of the Tree of the Knowledge of Good and Evil. If they did so, they would become aware of evil, which would lead to a desire not just to *know* good and evil, but to *determine* good and evil. Satan used our innate human preference to exert our own sovereignty to tempt Adam and Eve away from the communion with God we were created for and toward autonomy apart from God. Satan preyed upon their desire for autonomy. He told them they would not die when they ate the fruit, but would become *like God*. That's when the fruit became desirable. What God had said didn't matter anymore. Their desires and feelings usurped the truth. This seed of the post-truth mindset has bloomed in our day.

Fast-forward some millennia and we see another instance of post-truth. Two thousand years ago, during the most important trial of all time, Pontius Pilate, the governor of the Roman province of Judea, stood before Jesus and claimed the authority of the world's most powerful empire. Jesus stood before Pilate and claimed to be Truth incarnate. He declared that his authority and message weren't based on the vicissitudes of political power or cultural feelings, but on unchanging truth. "You say that I am a king," Jesus answered Pilate. "For this purpose I was born and for this purpose I have come into the world—to bear witness to the truth. Everyone who is of the truth listens to my voice" (John 18:37). Jesus handed Pilate the opportunity of the ages to ask a perfect follow-up question. The form of Pilate's next question was indeed perfect, but his motivation was anything but. "What is truth?" Pilate asked, walking away before Jesus could answer. It made for a dramatic exit, but a pitiful display. Pilate exchanged the opportunity of a lifetime for a rhetorical punch line. His attitude mirrors today's post-truth culture.

The 2004 motion picture *The Passion of the Christ* portrays a fictional yet scripturally consistent subsequent conversation between Pilate and his wife. Sitting in a now-empty court, Pilate sullenly asks his wife the same question he asked Jesus. "What is truth, Claudia? Do you hear it, recognize it when it is spoken?"

"Yes, I do. Don't you?"

"How? Can you tell me?"

She answers with a longtime spouse's candor. "If you will not hear the truth, no one can tell you." Steadfast in his cowardice, Pilate does not heed his wife's words, just as he failed to heed Jesus.

"Truth?" he snaps back. "Do you want to know what my truth is, Claudia? I've been putting down rebellions in this rotten outpost for eleven years. If I don't condemn this man, I know Caiaphas will start a rebellion. If I do condemn him, then his followers may. Either way, there will be bloodshed. Caesar has warned me, Claudia—warned me twice. He swore that the next time the blood would be mine. That is my truth!"[13]

Though Pilate uttered the word *truth* four times, he subordinated it to his personal situation and desires. He personalized the truth—calling it "my truth." Pilate wasn't a true skeptic. He was a cynic. A skeptic won't believe a truth claim until there is sufficient evidence. A cynic won't believe even if there is.

Pilate was a post-truth man, living with a post-truth mindset. He had the privilege of standing before the One who claimed to be Truth incarnate and would later prove it by rising from the dead. Yet Pilate wouldn't submit himself to the truth. He subordinated it to his personal preferences. How ironic that

Pilate's personal preferences trumped his recognition of a person who embodied Truth.

Jesus made the audacious claim that through him—and what he would accomplish on the cross—all of us could know the truth, and the truth would set us free (John 8:32). Some of us fervently hope Jesus was right about who he claimed to be. Others may prefer that Jesus was wrong in claiming to be the source of truth and true freedom. The most difficult step is realizing that our preferences aren't the governor here.

I understand the struggle between preference and truth acutely and so share something of a kinship with those who embrace a post-truth mindset. I was not born into a Christian background, yet today I follow Christ. In many ways, like the famous atheist convert C. S. Lewis, I desperately didn't want to meet the Jesus of the Bible. For most of my life I was a proud Muslim. I thought Islam was the truest path to paradise and every other worldview, especially Christianity, was wrong. But as I engaged with Christians about claims of Christ, I had the discomfort of uncovering what former Vice President Al Gore might call "an inconvenient truth." History, logic, and science pointed to the credibility of the Bible in general and to the claims of Christ in particular. My identity as a Muslim was at stake. Despite mounting evidence in favor of the Christian faith, I held onto the faith of my heritage because I preferred it, because I didn't want to change, because I preferred my side over the truth. Coming to embrace the truth about Jesus took me nine long years. It did not take me nine years to find the truth. It took me nine years to accept it. The truth wasn't hard to find, but it was hard to embrace. When I see today's post-truth snare, I know I was once caught in something similar.

As I once tried to avoid the Jesus of history, so our culture tries to avoid him. We may prefer a particular view about Jesus because it provides us with comfort, but what we need is the truth. "If you look for truth, you may find comfort in the end," C. S. Lewis wrote. "But if you look for comfort, you will not get either comfort or truth—only soft soap and wishful thinking to begin with and, in the end, despair."[14] Is the truth about Jesus more important than our preferences? Did Jesus give us proof that he alone can reliably guide us out of post-truth and into truth? The more post-truth spreads, the more desperately we need to know who can provide us with clarity. Having listened to many voices and examined many worldviews, I'm convinced that Jesus' voice is the truest.

Post-Truth's Full Bloom into the Culture of Confusion

Post-truth has now blossomed into a Culture of Confusion. Confusion is embraced as a virtue and clarity shunned as a sin. The answers to life's questions no longer need to correspond to reality. They need only cater to our desires.

But as our culture has embraced confusion and shunned clarity, have we found ourselves to be better off? The divisiveness of our rhetoric is corrosive. Those who disagree with us are "them." Facts often seem to be a problem to get around instead of the useful tools they once were. And if someone takes a stand we disagree with on a particular issue, we label them in the most uncharitable way possible, never mind whether they may have a point.

I remember the pervasive anxiety of the Cold War in the

1980s. The world worried that something would ignite tensions between the USA and USSR, initiating a nuclear war. The Cold War could suddenly become hotter than a thousand suns, quite literally. During that time, people in power claimed to know the way forward. Conservatives, liberals, moderates. Capitalists, socialists, communists, and anarchists. So many voices claimed to be able to lift us above it all. They did little to ease the anxiety. Popular musicians wrote a song about the "Land of Confusion."[15]

Thirty years later, do we not find ourselves neck-deep in the Land of Confusion? Men and women of power claim to be able to guarantee our unfettered freedoms, even it if may mean trampling on the freedoms of others. These same men and women of steel seem preoccupied with rights but often say very little about responsibilities. Yes, there are voices demanding truth and accuracy from our leaders, and rightfully so. But our demands for truth are so often selective—we want truth when it's convenient or when it supports our point of view. When we look at our world today and see all the questions being asked amid a culture not truly committed to sound answers, it's hard to imagine a land more confusing.

The confusion tends to swirl around certain questions: What does it mean to be human? What is human freedom and is it the same as autonomy? Do our rights have limits? Is there a transcendent meaning and purpose to human existence, or are we the measure of all things? We need clarity in our day to rightly answer these questions, to be informed individuals, honest scientists, and fair politicians. We need answers, not just questions. Yet as we ask questions, the Culture of Confusion's answers are inadequate and don't provide satisfaction. They don't bring us to dry land. The Culture of Confusion's answers only give birth to more questions. G. K. Chesterton presciently observed this phenomenon in his masterpiece *Orthodoxy*: "Free thought has exhausted its own freedom. It is weary of its own success." Thus, "we have found all of the questions that can be found. It is time we gave up looking for questions and began looking for answers."[16]

We need the unmovable to guide us if we are to find answers we can all live with. Blaise Pascal put it well: "When everything is moving at once, nothing appears to be moving, as on board ship. When everyone is moving towards depravity, no one seems to be moving. But if someone stops, he shows up the others who are rushing on, by acting as a fixed point."[17] There is one who stepped in the river of human history to provide an immovable fixed point of reference, even in the strongest of currents. In the pages that follow, I hope to demonstrate that it was not only Jesus' message in answering our deepest questions but also his actions that can bring clarity to a culture that needs it so desperately.

CHAPTER 2

Confusion and the Church: Seductions of a Post-Truth Mindset

There's an Arabic saying that often makes me smile: "*Kulna fil hawa sawa.*" It literally means "We're all in the same air," roughly conveying the same idea as the English saying, "We're all in the same boat." But Arabic sayings tend to have zestier connotations than their Western counterparts. "*Kulna fil hawa sawa*" really conveys the message, "We're all in the same stink," particularly the stink of the human condition. It's a pungent reminder that all of us—yes, all of us including Christians—have contributed to the Culture of Confusion's stench.

That's why, while this book is written to a wide audience, in this particular chapter I've fixed my gaze inwardly at my own community, specifically toward Christians. No book that addresses the trajectory of culture, especially the Culture of Confusion, would be fair without serious self-reflection about how every part of culture—including the one I'm in—contributes to both the stench and the aroma, the problem and the solution. And for that narrower audience, this chapter may sting the nostrils a bit.

If you're not a Christian, I offer two reasons for you to resist any temptation to skip this chapter. First, you'll learn how Christians have succumbed to the post-truth mindset similar to the way the rest of culture has. Second, it's always helpful to read an assessment of an influential part of the culture with which you don't identify. If you are a Christian, it's important to take a deep, sobering look at just how we may have contributed to the culture's confused state. To switch metaphors and to paraphrase Jesus, none of us—Christians or non-Christians—will have the credibility to remove the speck of confusion from our neighbor's eye until we've removed the post-truth log from our own.

The Imitation Game

In mid-2015, my news and social media feeds were abuzz with urgent-seeming headlines bemoaning, "It's Already Starting!" and "That Didn't Take Long!" The articles insinuated that an LGBT activist leveraged the United States Supreme Court's decision in *Obergefell v. Hodges* legalizing same-sex marriage to file a federal lawsuit to outlaw the Bible as hate speech.

Just three minutes of investigation revealed this narrative was bogus—and obviously so. Yes, a gay man filed a lawsuit in a Michigan federal court[1] against two Christian publishers. But he did not seek to have the Bible "banned." He sought money for emotional distress, claiming the publishers had mistranslated the Bible to be unfavorable to homosexuals. And he didn't file his lawsuit *after* the *Obergefell* decision. He filed it in 2008—seven years *before* the Supreme Court's ruling. Not only that, but the lawsuit was dismissed almost as soon as it was filed. The judge, a principled jurist I had the privilege of appearing before as an attorney, dismissed the case because it had no basis in the law and was "largely incomprehensible."

In less time than a TV commercial break, I learned that this alarmist story was false. And yet so many people were quick to believe an obviously untrue story and propel it to viral status. The irony saddened me because some of those who perpetuated the falsehood professed to follow Jesus, who claimed to be the very embodiment of truth (John 14:6). Whether the story was propagated by those who knew it was false or by those who were duped into believing it was true, the fact remains that Christians should have behaved differently. A common phrase in Christian circles is that the church is supposed to be "in but not of" the broader culture. In other words, Christians are to engage with the culture but not be unduly influenced by it. But so pervasive and seductive is the post-truth mindset that the church, at least to some degree, has become in *and* of the Culture of Confusion.

Part of this behavior is a reaction to society's growing perception of Christians as enemies of progress and freedom. Some Christians believe that battle lines have been drawn, which is why they get seduced into believing and spreading false stories about people they see to be the enemy. That's what makes the seductions of a post-truth Culture of Confusion all the more insidious. It plays on partial truths to goad us into believing and spreading untruths.

This is doubly sad because when the church has doubled down on its commitment to truth, especially in the face of opposition, it has flourished, brought credibility to the gospel, and benefited society. For Christians, now is not the time to be seduced into making "them" look as bad as possible while making "us" look as sympathetic as possible. Now is the time for compassionate, yet uncompromisingly expressed, truth. If the church's caving to the post-truth mindset has contributed to the larger cultural problem, then perhaps Christians' rediscovered commitment to the truth can lead us back to the solution.

Fixing What Bugs Us

Not long ago I spoke at a major university in Canada on the topic "Disagreeing Without Being Disagreeable." A member of the audience took to the microphone to pose an interesting question. "I'm a software engineer," he began. "Once we've designed the software, we test it for things that bug us about it. Not just glitches, but things about the software we personally don't like. If you were to do the same test on the church, what would bug you about it?"

The audience nervously laughed at the hot-seat question. How would I, as someone who's spoken at many churches around the world, respond? While I think the church is doing great things locally and across the world, there are things that could use changing.[2] But first we have to understand what we're hoping to debug when we reference "the church." Consider the fact that many people today, still the vast majority in the United States, call themselves Christians. But donning a label doesn't equate to being the genuine article. Peering behind the veils, we see that only three out of ten Americans are practicing Christians, meaning that Christian living, Bible reading, and regular church attendance are important to their lives.[3] And given that America is still more religious than most European countries, Australia, or Canada, it's safe to say that an even smaller percentage of people in Western countries are practicing Christians. "Legacy Christians," as Dave Kinnaman and Gabe Lyons call them, are those for whom Christianity is "background noise that can safely be ignored."[4] While "three out of four U.S. adults have some Christian background . . . about three in five American Christians are largely inactive in their faith."[5] Given these numbers, the sensationalistic or false stories purveyed in the trending social media posts come largely—but not solely—from people for whom being Christian is little more than a moniker that distinguishes them from politically left-leaning people.

Who I want to address here are practicing Christians— men and women for whom Christianity is a way of life, regular church attendance is their practice, and devotion to Jesus is their ultimate aim. When I refer to the church from now on in this chapter, that is who I mean. Although practicing Christians are less influenced by the Culture of Confusion, the influence is significant enough that we have to address it. So to root out the bugs, we have to start there.

Seduction in Two-Part Harmony

The church has succumbed to post-truth's soft expression in two seemingly contrary ways. On one hand, Christians have compromised the clarity of Scripture for the sake of acceptance and to avoid conflict. On the other hand, Christians have indulged the cultural practice of vilifying those with whom they disagree. These two seductions seem contradictory, but when they work together, they harmonize in a grisly dirge.

Let's address the first post-truth seduction: making the gospel pill easier to swallow to avoid uncomfortable discussions with non-Christians and difficult Bible passages that challenge our behavioral preferences. In our effort to be liked, Jesus' famous statement, "Judge not lest ye be judged," is often misquoted. Many, including those in the church, interpret this passage to mean that Jesus shunned moral judgment. And, so the argument goes, Christians have no place judging the actions of others in the broader culture. It's quite telling that so few people quote the entire context of Jesus' words. The full passage reads:

> "Judge not, that you be not judged. For with the judgment you pronounce you will be judged, and with the measure you use it will be measured to you. Why do you see the speck that is in your brother's eye, but do not notice the log that is in your own eye? Or how can you say to your brother, 'Let me take the speck out of your eye,' when there is the log in your own eye? You hypocrite, first take the log out of your own eye, and then you will see clearly to take the speck out of your brother's eye." (Matthew 7:1–5)

It's worth pausing for a moment to see just how Jesus' words actually express a message opposite to what so many want him to have expressed. Jesus says that when we remove the log from our own eye, we will see clearly how to judge our brother's actions. Applied today, if the church gets the post-truth speck out of its own eye, it can bring clarity to a world of confusion. In the full context, we see that Jesus is saying that when we judge, it is to be for the improvement of others, not their condemnation.

So why do so many people, including Christians, misapply Jesus' statements as a blanket prohibition against all judgment? There are as many reasons as there are people who do so. One common reason is that Christians want to appear tolerant and likable, especially in a time when tolerance—though woefully misdefined—is a chief virtue. Put plainly, many Christians have bought into what Kinnaman and Lyons call "the new moral code" that people should not criticize someone else's life choices. Can we see the seduction playing out right before our eyes? The post-truth Culture of Confusion elevates preferences and feelings over facts and truth. And by elevating our preferences to be liked and feel accepted, Christians have misapplied the plain truth of Jesus' words and exchanged them for pleasant cultural comforts. This brings to mind Dallas Willard's apt assessment of the spiritual landscape, in which "most of what Americans do in their religion now is done at the behest of feelings. . . . The quest for pleasure takes over the house of God."[6] Willard's indictment is true for some of us all of the time. And it is true for all of us at least some of the time.

The second seduction—that of using the truths of Scripture to bludgeon outsiders—brings a pendular swing of overcorrecting our desire to be liked. Too often, Christians conveniently forget the fact that like everyone else, they need a Savior. When Christians forget that, they create an "us versus them" paradigm leading to Christians hungrily gobbling up and passing along iffy articles about how awful "they" are without a moment's pause. Worse yet, Christians may make churches so unwelcoming that they repel the very people who could benefit from what Jesus has to offer. Truth is once again sacrificed, but this time at the altar of a self-righteous higher agenda to stand up to "them." Fair or not, people judge the credibility of a message by the integrity of the messenger. If the gospel message of compassion, forgiveness, and reconciliation is proclaimed by those who seem to have none of those qualities, it's hard to see how the broader culture's response can be anything but concomitant dismay and anger.

Dancing to a Different Tune

The way forward tempers both our need to be liked and the importance of addressing detrimental ideas and behaviors. A story in Marie Chapian's book *Of Whom the World Was Not Worthy* comes to mind. She recounts the story of Jakob, a missionary to the former Yugoslavia, who encounters Cimmerman, a farmer who had lost much to the country's rampant violence and corruption. When Jakob tried to share the gospel message with him, Cimmerman would have none of it. Angered by the clergy's complicity in the ugliness, Cimmerman refused to hear Jakob out. "Those men of the cloth tortured and killed my own nephew before my eyes," he spewed. "I saw him die in his own blood, and then I watched the killers calmly genuflect before the main altar of the church, cross themselves with holy water, and a few moments later their forks scraped their plates as they ate their supper in the parish house."[7] Obviously, Cimmerman's reaction had nothing to do with the gospel message's truth or falsity. Church corruption does not change the facts of Jesus' death and resurrection. But the point is this: Cimmerman dismissed the message (indeed, he dismissed Christ himself) based on his experiences with those who claimed to believe the message.

Today's Cimmermans distrust Christians as ultraconservative, hypocritical judging exclusivists. That is, of course, a sweeping and unfair characterization. Nevertheless, that perception persists and even grows. The broader culture hears Christians lament the erosion of marriage while believing that Christians divorce at the same rate as non-Christians. (They do not, but that is a common misperception.)[8] Non-Christians see Christians supporting conservative political leaders regardless of their sometimes serious moral failings, yet condemning liberal leaders for those same failings. While I think this mischaracterizes most genuine Christians, there are those louder-than-normal voices within the church who judge with unmitigated bias and give full vent to their anger at outsiders, "those people," without reflecting on their own sin.

The church can recapture its positive cultural influence if it rekindles its passion for the principles that revolutionized the world so long ago. In sharp contrast to our current adversarial attitudes, Jesus told us to love our enemies and to pray for those who persecute us (Matthew 5:44). Christians are to be "the salt of the earth" and "the light of the world" (Matthew 5:13–14). But if the church sees everyone as enemies to be vanquished, it will lose its savor and its brightness. What we need is neither complacency nor indignation. What we need is wisdom.

A Wise Temperament: Cooling the Smoldering Anger

The book of Proverbs provides a template for how Christians can once again be as savory as salt and illuminating as light in a bitter and dark time. If there is a word other than *confused* to describe the current cultural mood, it has to be *angry*. From protests that flare up at a moment's notice to knee-jerk branding others with epithets, we seem to have lost our ability to be civil to one another in the thick of debate. And there seem to be fewer and fewer exceptions in either secular or religious circles. And yet, thankfully, I experienced some refreshing exceptions recently.

I was blessed with the opportunity to speak at an open forum alongside Ravi Zacharias at my alma mater, the University of Michigan, on the topic "What Does It Mean to Be Human?" Every one of the 3,500 seats at Hill Auditorium was filled by atheists, agnostics, Christians, and people from different religious faiths. During the question-and-answer period, an erudite young man identifying himself as an atheist opened his question with an interesting comment: "I first want to thank the university for allowing this event to happen on campus so that we can hear and interact with differing viewpoints. I didn't see any cars on fire or broken windows." Of course, he was referring to recent incidents at the University of California at Berkeley where protestors ignited fires and damaged property in reaction to a lightning rod speaker who had come to that campus. In the weeks surrounding the Berkeley incident, the news was awash with similar stories at other prestigious universities. In March 2017, students at Middlebury College in Vermont protested a speech by controversial scholar Charles Murray. The protest erupted into physical assaults against both Murray and a Middlebury faculty member, leaving her with a twisted neck and a visit to the ER.

The stunning applicability of ages-old biblical wisdom shows how holy writ remains eternally contemporary. In Proverbs 29,

Solomon wrote that "Scoffers set a city aflame, but the wise turn away wrath. . . . A fool gives full vent to [anger], but [the] wise . . . quietly holds it back" (Prov. 29:8, 11). At Berkeley, Middlebury College, and other similar institutions, some protesters gave full vent to their anger, yet those protests could have happened without mayhem and violence.

Contrast has a way of clarifying things, as author Os Guinness would say. Our open forum at the University of Michigan had its share of challenging questions. In fact most of the questions came from skeptics. The evening was lively, yet civil. The students didn't shut us down; they engaged with ideas they may not have agreed with. And thankfully Ravi and I were able to articulate our Christian positions on life's biggest questions without compromise, all the while holding each questioner's dignity as sacrosanct. Happily, that same civility carried over to an even bigger crowd the next day at Michigan State University and again the following week at Indiana University. We were able to disagree because we intended to do so agreeably. In the days following those events, we had the pleasure of seeing some who started out disagreeing end up agreeing and embracing the gospel. Weeks before taking the podiums at those schools, we prayed specifically for ears to be sensitive, tongues to be judicious, and hearts to be compassionate. Again, in the wise words of Solomon, "Whoever restrains his words has knowledge, and he who has a cool spirit is a man of understanding" (Prov. 17:27).

Let's pause once more for self-assessment. Lest Christians think that Solomon's wisdom applies only to others, we must remember that in the Culture of Confusion, we are as susceptible to the kind of anger that erupted at Berkeley, Middlebury, and elsewhere. As I write this, I've just read a message from a Christian friend lamenting how Christians cast aside Solomon's advice and accosted both him and a Muslim for just having a calm conversation about their different religious beliefs. The group of Christians began yelling at the Muslim for being a "liar" and my friend for being a "charlatan" just because he refused to polemicize the discussion. In the Culture of Confusion, it's seductively easy for any one of us to turn civility into a vice.

What a contrast to the attitude the apostle Paul passed down to his protégé Titus. "Remind them . . . to speak evil of no one, to avoid quarreling, to be gentle, and to show perfect courtesy toward all people" (Titus 3:1–2). Paul wasn't against engaging in reasoned argument, but he was against quarreling, especially the kind that results in vilifying someone else. Why is it so important for Christians to speak evil of no one (yes, *no one*) and to show perfect courtesy toward all people (yes, *all* people)? Because the gospel message teaches that all of us are broken people, given to sin, anger, and even hatred. Those who claim allegiance to Christ are to be washed of such things, not by their own goodness, but by God's mercy and grace. As Paul continues, "For we ourselves were once foolish, disobedient, led astray, slaves to various passions and pleasures, passing our days in malice and envy, hated by others and hating one another" (v. 3).

One wonders if the people who accosted my friend and the Muslim he was chatting with had taken time to reflect on Paul's words before giving full vent to their anger. What result did they expect? Did they expect the Muslim to suddenly drop all of his deeply held convictions because the decibel level had increased? Or, more likely, did they expect to set the situation aflame and bring heat, not light? Thankfully, my friend stayed in the conversation and nurtured his friendship with the Muslim. It is when we have a cool spirit, turn away wrath, and withhold our anger that our words—the message of the gospel of peace and clarity— can be heard. Students heard the gospel at the universities we visited because we were able to express our convictions without degrading anyone. And, thankfully, my friend was able to share his beliefs because he saw a person, not a target. With this kind of renewal and regeneration, Christians can—and should— speak with conviction and courage in the face of opposition, but we must do so in a way that recognizes that "we" were once— and in some ways still are—"them."

Wise Words: The Truth, the Whole Truth, and Nothing But the Truth

I often remind myself of another popular saying: "It is better to remain silent and be thought a fool than to open your mouth and remove all doubt." That contemporary idiom is a paraphrase of Solomon's centuries-old advice: "The tongue of the wise commends knowledge, but the mouths of fools pour out folly" (Prov. 15:2).

Today it's not only incredibly easy to broadcast our opinions or spread dubious stories, it's also fashionable to do so hastily. With the advent of YouTube, Twitter, Facebook (a digital triumvirate my colleague Michael Ramsden calls "YouTwitFace"), and other social media platforms, everyone has become a journalist. But few of us take the time to verify our sources. This is true of the wider culture and sadly of Christians as well. Recall the Bible lawsuit discussed above. That was fake news, plain and simple, propagated at a breakneck pace by those bearing the name Christian. When we hear the term "the speed of light," we think of the fastest something can travel. But in the social media age, perhaps we should change the phrase to "the speed of lies."

Thankfully, there are many Christians who take great pains to share accurate stories and engage honestly with others. When they do, they emulate another biblical proverb: "One who walks in integrity will be safe, but whoever follows crooked ways will fall into the Pit" (Prov. 28:18, NRSV). Integrity is the key word here, and we desperately need more of it. Integrity takes years to build and only moments to destroy. With all of the misinformation and disinformation, it would be easy to say that we should abandon the whole enterprise of social media engagement. Judging by the hunched gazes I observe at airports, though, social media use doesn't appear to be fading. If Christians are to meaningfully contribute to the cultural conversation through social media, they must do so with integrity.[9]

Now the temptation is to quickly spread stories that uphold Christian views and values (perhaps even with some exaggerations) because "the other side" allegedly spreads misinformation so quickly that we have to level the playing field regardless of which "side" we're on. That tactic is emblematic of what the post-truth Culture of Confusion is all about. It must not be the church's teacher.

When our digital or verbal discussions lack integrity, there are consequences beyond mere misinformation. The shrapnel of our hasty and angry explosions wound real people. Christian social commentator Ed Stetzer called his fellow Christians to account for perpetuating a debunked conspiracy theory about the tragic death of Seth Rich, who once worked for the Democratic National Committee.[10] The barrage of conspiracy theories that followed his murder forced Seth Rich's parents to relive the tragedy. In their anguished words, "With every conspiratorial flare-up, we are forced to relive Seth's murder and a small piece of us dies as more of Seth's memory is torn away from us."[11]

It's a deep enough wound to bury your child. To have your memories of him stripped of sentimentality because of political machinations inflicts a deeper wound yet. Regardless of your politics or your religion, the Rich family's waking nightmare ought to give us pause before we carelessly click "share" even one more time. Indeed, Jesus' words on this point are direct and convicting: "On the day of judgment you will have to give an account for every careless word you utter; for by your words you will be justified, and by your words you will be condemned" (Matthew 12:36–37 NRSV).

Those should be soul-shuddering words for followers of Christ. Words are meant to convey truth and bring life, not peddle falsehood or foster pain. That's why God judges careless words so severely. In Christ, God himself is the Word made flesh (John 1:1, 14). If Christians are his ambassadors, then they are called to carefully choose their words. Do our words convey truth? Do they convey life? Only then will our words be wise and clear in a Culture of Confusion.

Anger isn't necessarily opposed to wise and compassionate words. When exercised with wisdom and restraint, anger can lead to positive change. Greed, racial discrimination, sexual harassment, and other injustices ought to anger us. But may I say that anger, even if legitimate, can become sinful if

unchecked by godly love for others and for the truth? Anger—
even when directed at the appropriate things—can be sinful
if it causes us to sacrifice clarity and truth for the sake of self-
vindication. Susanna Wesley, famed preacher John Wesley's
mother, wisely taught her children about sin's invidious creep
into even our most legitimate motivations: "Whatever weak-
ens your reason, impairs the tenderness of your conscience,
obscures your sense of God, or takes off your relish of spiritual
things: in short, whatever increases the strength and authority
of your body over your mind, that thing is sin to you, *however
innocent it may be in itself.*" [12]

We would do well to heed her words. Our indignation over
the deterioration of the culture may be legitimate, but it can
lead to sinful bitterness. Our anger over sickness, poverty, and
moral decay may lead us to act, but it can also ensnare us into
caring more about causes than about the people those causes
were meant to help. That's the fundamental danger inherent in failing to wisely use words. When we dance with the
post-truth Culture of Confusion, the culture doesn't change.
It changes us, and not for the better. When we are so eager
to believe the worst about others, we bring out the worst in
ourselves. C. S. Lewis warned us against letting that darkness
creep in:

> Suppose one reads a story of filthy atrocities in the
> paper. Then suppose that something turns up suggesting
> that the story might not be quite true, or not quite so bad
> as it was made out. Is one's first feeling, "Thank God, even
> they aren't quite so bad as that," or is it a feeling of disap-
> pointment, and even a determination to cling to the first

story for the sheer pleasure of thinking your enemies are as bad as possible? If it is the second then it is, I am afraid, the first step in a process which, if followed to the end, will make us into devils.[13]

We may see ourselves reflected in Lewis's words more than we care to. May we rise above such heart-clouding cynicism. May the church have a wise temperament that leads to wise words saturated with integrity and tempered with grace. And may those wise words lead to wise actions.

Wise Actions: Caring for the Culture

A central Christian principle is that all people are made in the image of God. Accordingly, all people must be treated with dignity and respect even (especially) when their ideas or behaviors challenge us or must be challenged by us. In Jesus' day, a teacher of the law challenged him to identify which commandment was the greatest. "You shall love the Lord your God with all your heart and with all your soul and with all your mind. This is the great and first commandment." He continued, "And a second is like it: You shall love your neighbor as yourself. On these two commandments depend all the Law and the Prophets" (Matthew 22:37–40). Jesus emphasized loving God and loving the people he created.

It's fascinating that Jesus paired the command to love people with the command to love God. The legal scholars of his day would have thought this to be a blasphemous elevation of humanity. But Jesus did so because the person challenging him was a Pharisee, one who had dedicated his life to following all 613 laws in the Torah, but who had forgotten about caring for others in the process. In other words, in his zeal to express his love of God, he failed to love people. And in doing so, he actually failed to truly love God. One cannot love God but fail to love the people he created. That doesn't require unconditional agreement or affirmation with everything a person believes or does. But it does entail compassion for that person.

That love has motivated Christians historically. Paul Lee Tan expressed that "a Christian is a mind through which Christ thinks, a heart through which Christ loves, a mouth through which Christ speaks, a hand through which Christ helps."[14] In the days of the Roman Empire, both before and after Emperor Constantine's conversion, Christians founded hospitals to care for all the people who needed help. And it was Christians, suffering under tremendous persecution in the Roman Empire, who aided the Roman pagans and bound their wounds nevertheless. As David Bentley Hart explains, "Even the [pagan] emperor Julian, who was all too conscious of the hypocrisies of which Christians are capable, was forced to lament, in a letter to a pagan priest, 'It is a disgrace that these impious Galileans care not only for their own poor but for ours as well.'"[15] From the second century through the fourteenth and beyond, Christians rushed into plague-infected areas to aid the sick and dying while others fled, sometimes dying from the plague themselves. It was Christians who led the charge in England and the United States to end the vile slave trade.

Mark Twain is credited as saying, "History doesn't repeat, but it sure does rhyme." Today, although there are good secular and non-Christian organizations making a difference,

Christians often still lead the way. From starting universities like Harvard, Oxford, and others to founding hospitals, to caring for the sick in Ebola-stricken West Africa only to contract Ebola themselves, those Christians whose actions are consistent with their words are helping to change the hearts of the very people who once opposed them. The coupling of wise words and wise actions doesn't just get things done, it gets things—and people—changed. Matthew Parris, the well-known atheist, describes how the gospel message outpaces secular efforts to change the desperate situation in his African homeland. In an article entitled "As an Atheist, I Truly Believe Africa Needs God," Parris wrote that secular "education and training alone will not do. In Africa, Christianity changes people's hearts. It brings a spiritual transformation. *The rebirth is real. The change is good.*"[16]

Pause for a moment on the paradoxical depth of Parris's carefully chosen words. He's saying the Christian *message* has made the difference in Africa. That message is at once about the depravity of every human heart and the dignity of every human being. History indeed has rhymed. And when the gospel is the central chorus, the melody can be beautiful.

Wearing the Truth as a Coat

And so we return to Jakob and Cimmerman. Jakob had tried to share the gospel with Cimmerman, and Cimmerman resisted by pointing out that the corrupt church leaders wore their fancy clothes and holy garments to conceal the filthiness of their hearts.

Jakob posed a question to the embittered Cimmerman.

He asked Cimmerman to suppose that someone had stolen his coat and boots and then robbed someone. What would Cimmerman say when the authorities came to arrest him as the misidentified perpetrator because the robber wore his stolen coat? Obviously, he would say that someone had stolen his coat, pretending to be him. Still unmoved, Cimmerman replied, "I do not believe in the name of your God."

In the ensuing year, Jakob cultivated a friendship with Cimmerman. Cracks formed in Cimmerman's stony veneer. He not only heard Jakob's words but saw his temperament and benefited from his kindness. One day, looking at his friend through tearful eyes, Cimmerman expressed his newfound love of Jesus. He told Jakob, "You wear his coat well."[17]

The post-truth Culture of Confusion is angry at Christians and rejects the message we carry. We must honestly assess our part in perpetuating the confusion and fomenting the anger. Centuries after Solomon, the apostle Paul wrote that when Christians encounter non-Christians, we are to be wise. "Let your speech always be gracious, seasoned with salt," Paul tells us, "so that you may know how you ought to answer each person" (Col. 4:6). Notice that Paul didn't say that we are to answer each question, challenge, controversy, or political issue. We are to answer people. Questions and controversies don't need answers. People do.

The confusion and anger swirling about can be daunting. But if we have integrity and courage, we can change perceptions of the church and the gospel it carries. Integrity is the currency of truth. Courage is its backbone. When we adopt both, and perhaps only then, can the church wear Jesus' coat well for all to see.

CHAPTER 3

Confusion's Consequences— Getting Freedom Wrong

From quite a distance I could hear the shouting directly in my path. On my way to a midafternoon class at the University of Michigan, I was crossing the "Diag," the main square in central campus where two busy paths diagonally converged in an "X"—hence the name. As I drew closer, it became clear that I wasn't about to witness an argument or some kind of protest. I could see that a small crowd had surrounded a man, obviously not a student, who was doing all the shouting. Words like "Jesus," "sinner," and "Savior" became more discernible as he filled the crisp autumn air with his impressive lungs. Despite the usual gray late-autumn chill, "Preacher Mike" didn't need a jacket. With all of his hand-waving and shouting, he was practically sweating.

Other than Preacher Mike's body heat, no other heat was generated. I'd heard street preachers with similar messages before, but this time I paused to see how the other students were reacting. Most just stood and listened briefly before heading off. Some engaged him in passionate yet respectful disagreement. A few would just walk by and squawk something like, "Go home, wacko!" But no one tried to silence Preacher Mike.

In fact, I would have been shocked if someone did. In my experience, college in the early '90s was expected to be a place of freedom, not only from parentally instituted curfews but also for expression of and engagement with different—even disagreeable—ideas. The original spirit of university, where faculty and students gathered in a unified place (Latin *unum*) to discover truth (*veritas*), was alive.

Looking back, I see that the political correctness movement was beginning to encroach on that original university spirit. Things were already headed toward today's intolerant "tolerance." In just one generation's time, the university has become a chief arena in which freedom to share differing opinions is decaying. How anti-university it is that Western colleges make headlines because someone's right to speak is shouted down or, in some cases, met with violence.

Courting Chaos: Confusing Autonomy for Freedom

We won't explore free speech's foundations here. Rather, we need to understand the foundations for freedom itself because freedom has become a confused concept today. The current climate, in which people are forcibly prevented from sharing ideas, has arisen because we have mistaken *autonomy* for *freedom*. They are related but different concepts. In a post-truth culture, where preferences and opinions are elevated over facts and truth, anything that challenges our preferences, even if a challenge is laced with facts, is deemed offensive and oppressive. How dare someone disagree with my preferences or opinions? Isn't freedom found in being able to fully express one's preferences and opinions without challenge? Western freedom is all about the ability to do, feel, and say whatever we want so long as we don't hurt someone else, isn't it? Even if we do hurt someone else, it's only because that someone else isn't affirming our preferences. And that person is an oppressor anyway. If oppressors get hurt in the process, well, they had it coming. Freedom must have no bounds. Not even reality will be our boundary.

But what I've just described isn't freedom—it's autonomy. While we typically understand freedom to be the power to exercise choice without constraint, as we'll soon see, freedom becomes chaotic in a system without constraint. Freedom operates at its best within the confines of the truth. Boundaries are foreign to pure autonomy, which means that truth is being sacrificed on autonomy's altar.

The word *autonomy* is comprised of two root words from Greek. The first root word is *autos*, meaning "self," and the second is *nomos*, meaning "law." Someone is autonomous if he is a law unto himself. And the pursuit of autonomy—not freedom—is what we are seeing today. I would argue that the pursuit of autonomy is the root of the post-truth mindset that fuels the Culture of Confusion. We have been pursuing autonomy since the beginning of our race. Adam and Eve sought autonomy from God. They sought to transcend the purpose for which they were made so that they could be the definers of their own purpose. We continue that pursuit today.

What is the natural result of the unfettered autonomy we seek? Everything becomes subject to our personal preferences, even our pursuit of truth. Jens Zimmermann points out that "we approach knowledge the way teenagers approach parental authority: 'no one tell me what to think.' . . . Consequently, we lump together tradition, Authority and indoctrination, equate them with coercion and reject any intrusion on the pure slate of our autonomous minds."[1] If each of our personal preferences is celebrated without truth as our guide, if we are all "laws unto ourselves," confusion is inevitable. When my law unto myself conflicts with another's law unto himself, what can arbitrate between us if not truth? When truth is sacrificed as the burnt offering on the altar of autonomy, the resultant smoke chokes the breath out of freedom. Only chaos remains, which ultimately leads to bondage.

The First Sacrifice: Our Ability to Reason

The initial detritus that falls next to the altar of autonomy is our ability to think and act clearly and wisely. An incident at the University of Missouri comes to mind. In 2015, football players protested the handling of racist incidents on campus by Timothy Wolfe, the university's president. Naturally, this attracted media attention, especially from sports media outlets. ESPN commissioned a photojournalist who was also a student to take pictures. But the journalist made the mistake of taking photos of athletes while in a so-called "safe space"—safe from media attention. The entire incident was recorded on a bystander's phone and put on YouTube. The video shows an angry professor who was taking part in the protest confronting that photojournalist and calling for "muscle" to forcibly remove him. More surprising is that the professor who wanted to forcibly remove the student journalist was a communications professor associated with the school of journalism. What a stark illustration of our post-truth Culture of Confusion. A professor whose area of study depends on the freedom of the press sought to suppress a journalist's right to cover a protest of public interest. Only feeling-driven irrationality can lead a communications professor to try to forcibly remove a photojournalist from a media-hungry protest, all in the name of safeguarding student preferences for a safe space.

That kind of irrationality seems to be cropping up elsewhere. In late 2015, Yale University administrators issued guidelines cautioning students against wearing Halloween costumes that might be culturally offensive to some students. If a white student dressed as a samurai, for example, that could be deemed an offensive cultural appropriation. One Yale educator, Erika Christakis, pushed back. She penned a graciously worded email expressing her understanding for cultural sensitivity but also her unease that the university guidelines might suppress student expression. She did not get the reaction she expected.

Students, the very people whose freedom of expression Christakis sought to protect, were incensed that she dared to champion a path that might lead to offensive conduct. Her husband, Professor Nicholas Christakis, tried to defend her position. Seeking to calm the clamor for his wife's job, he listened to the angered students' concerns. He was not met with a commensurately listening ear. They shouted him down, telling other students to "walk away. He doesn't deserve to be listened to." The students demanded that Erika and Nicholas Christakis resign their respective positions.

That outrage displays the decay of reasoning, even among our intellectual elite, brought on by a post-truth culture. Nicholas Christakis was the Master of Yale's Silliman Residential College. As such, he was charged with living in the dorms to help shape the residents' cultural, emotional, and intellectual lives. But when the same students' preferences to avoid anything offensive clashed with the right to free expression, reason and truth no longer guided the discussions. One student shouted at Christakis, "It's your job to create a place of comfort and home for the students who live in Silliman. You have not done that. By sending out that email, that goes against your position as master. Do you understand that!?" When he dared to calmly disagree, Nicholas Christakis was pummeled with invective. After exploding with expletives, a student shouted, "You should step down! If that is what you think about being a master, you should step down! It is *not* about creating an intellectual space! It is *not!* Do you understand that? It's about creating a home here. You are not doing that!"[2]

Notice what happened. Christakis's job as a master at Yale was to ensure the social, cultural, and intellectual life of the students at Silliman College. Specifically, a master at Yale "is responsible for . . . fostering and shaping the social, cultural, and *educational* life and character of the college. During the year, he or she hosts *lectures*, study breaks (especially during finals), and College Teas—intimate gatherings during which students have the opportunity to engage with renowned guests from the *academy, government, or popular culture*" (emphases mine).[3] By trying to discuss the interplay of free expression and cultural sensitivity, he attempted to serve all of those goals. Yet the student shouted that Christakis's job was *not* about creating an intellectual space, even though it is part of the description of a master's job.

The truth was that the Christakises *did* have an obligation to create an intellectual space for the students to challenge each other. The truth is that universities should foster free expression, even if disagreeable or crass. But those students preferred to be safe from such truths. The unfortunate irony is that Erika Christakis wrote her email to safeguard the students' *freedom*. But the competing autonomous desire—to be safe from anything remotely offensive—clashed with freedom. And in a culture where autonomous preferences and feelings prevail over facts, two professors who had the students' best interests at heart eventually had to resign as masters at Silliman College, though both remain professors at Yale.[4]

How can reason survive in such a climate? When we vaunt feelings over facts in our quest for autonomy, reason dies. One is reminded of the words of Thomas Sowell: "The problem isn't that Johnny can't read or even that Johnny can't think. It's that Johnny doesn't know what thinking is. He's confused it with feeling."[5]

The quest for autonomy has led us down an endless road with no traffic lights or painted lines. And as we hitchhike along that road, we may jump into a car that's going partly our way, only to kick out the driver after he's served our purpose. Take, for example, the recent cultural focus on transgenderism.

There are people who experience genuine gender dysphoria—a diagnosable condition where one's pervasive psychological feeling of gender is incongruous with one's anatomical sex. Such people languish in the disparity between their minds and their bodies and may or may not seek to change their anatomy. Yet what we're seeing today, with over fifty different gender identities that were once available for our Facebook profiles,[6] has everything to do with human autonomy and nearly nothing to do with a genuine, pain-filled struggle. Those who want no limits on who or what they are, not even biological or psychological limits, have turned those who have genuine struggles into the poster children for the quest for autonomy. Never mind that gender dysphoric people largely wish they weren't. Never mind that a large number of those who elect sex reassignment surgery still feel depressed and succumb to suicide at shockingly high rates.[7] Those are just statistics, after all, and we have our unrestrained autonomy to think of. If the facts get in the way of it, well, the facts will have to be ignored and any opposition will be silenced.

But there are real people at issue, not just statistics. Stories are cropping up of biologically male athletes competing in women's events alongside women, breaking records. How long before males start vying for the athletic scholarships now open to women or winning positions on women's teams? The equal opportunities secured by federal law for women to fairly compete in sports will simply erode away. Women who were once top athletes among their peers must compete even harder for rights they thought they had already won. Such women aren't statistics. Yet they, along with common sense, are sacrificed on autonomy's altar. We no longer just elevate personal preferences over truth. We elevate our particular preferences over the preferences of others. With the soft version of post-truth, the facts don't matter. Nor do other people's preferences. Only *my* preferences matter. In the quest for autonomy, some facts may be undeniable, but our autonomy is undebatable.

One thinks of the viral YouTube video of an adult, Caucasian, five-foot-six-inch man who asked University of Washington students what they would say if he told them he was a six-foot-five-inch, seven-year-old Chinese girl. Though some showed discomfort, not one of the students denied his ridiculous self-identifications. Juxtaposing those students with the Yale students puts the depth of our cultural confusion into perspective. At Yale, the students were exercised because the Christakises' favoring of free expression might encourage cultural appropriation. But at the University of Washington, students affirmed a white man's self-identification as a young Chinese girl. It should seem obvious that identifying as a person from a completely different ethnicity appropriates far more of a culture than wearing a Halloween costume. Yet the former was affirmed and the latter vilified. Why? Because the magic words "I identify" preceded an outrageous claim, thereby rendering the appropriation inoffensive. The famed pop singer Miley Cyrus made the audacious claim to be a pansexual, genderless, ageless spirit. "I think I feel genderless, I feel ageless," she says. "I'm just a spirit soul not divided by human beings, even animals. There's no me and them and there's no us and you. I just want to be nothing."[8] Despite the patent illogic of that statement, she seems to be singing it in harmony with our autonomy-driven culture.

Similar support is strangely absent when it comes to

extremists who kill in the name of Islam. When extremists who identify as Muslims commit an atrocity, many are quick to say that those terrorists aren't real Muslims; they have hijacked the religion to serve their homicidal and political ends. But wait, they *identify* as Muslims, so how can we justify denying their self-identifications? Is it because the terrorists are bad people? Do only morally upstanding people get to pick who and what they are? And who has the authority to determine whether another person is moral enough to have their self-identification validated? The whole enterprise of self-identification has become arbitrary—especially given that religion is a matter of personal choice that transcends sex, race, ethnicity, and geography.

My point is not to argue whether Islam is inherently peaceful or not, or whether Muslims are peaceful on the whole, as most of them are. My point is to reveal the illogical schizophrenia that underlies our autonomy-obsessed Culture of Confusion. Many say that violent extremists are not true Muslims and marshal evidence to argue that these killers' atrocities are inconsistent with "true" Islam. Such statements are considered noble and tolerant. But when someone tries to show that another's gender, racial, or ethnic self-identification is contrary to the clear evidence, that's seen as ignoble and bigoted. What can explain this disconnect other than the atrophy of our ability to reason?

This chaos highlights our need for the very consistency that's bleeding to death under our preference-driven knives. Logical consistency necessitates that we examine evidence and compare it to someone's identity claims. I would hate to be on the receiving end of someone's misattribution of identity despite the facts. If someone commits an atrocity in the name of Christ (history has had its unfortunate fill of such people), I hope that we would ask ourselves whether that person's beliefs or actions are consistent with Jesus' teachings. I would hope that anyone would make the same inquiry, should it pertain to someone claiming to be a Muslim, a Buddhist, a woman, a man, six-feet-five inches tall, or Chinese. A truth-based inquiry might be difficult and painful, but greater difficulty and pain will follow if it is abandoned.

I'm trained as a lawyer, a profession whose emphasis on linguistic accuracy and precision isn't merely academic but a matter of justice or injustice. In California and in Canada, it has become punishable to refer to someone by a gender noun or pronoun that isn't of their choosing. With so many choices, it may be difficult to enforce that law. Worse yet, it may be too easy to enforce it if someone can be considered guilty just for repeatedly getting a pronoun wrong. With the contemporary push to get away from gender-specific pronouns, how can the legal system work properly? It may matter how many people were present at a meeting or how many people witnessed a suspect's alibi. But if we employ vague gender terms like "they" or "zhi" or "zher" to reference a single person, will a jury become confused? In fact, the *New York Times* fell victim to that confusion, having to issue a correction of a list originally intended to clarify the many gender-neutral pronouns:

> Correction: February 8, 2015. A chart on Page 20 this weekend with an article about gender identity at the University of Vermont renders four gender-neutral pronouns incorrectly. The pronouns are zirs and zirself, not zis and zieself (for his/hers and himself/herself); sir, not sie (for him/her); and eirself, not emself (for himself/herself).[9]

The clarification is as confusing as the original mistake. If a mainstream, influential newspaper like the *New York Times*—with reporters dedicated to getting the facts right—can't untangle the thorny brambles, can a jury be relied upon to do so? Furthermore, isn't it foreseeable that a person would repeatedly get another person's chosen gender pronoun wrong, especially if they change it later? Confusion in courtrooms can have real consequences, not just in potentially harming our judicial system but also real victims of real crimes.

Indeed, de-gendering language is actually ethnocentric and imperialistic. While English may not be gender based, many other languages of the world are. The tongue of my heritage, Arabic, has feminine and masculine nouns, adjectives, and verb conjugations. The same goes for Farsi, French, Spanish, Italian, and hundreds of other languages. They are based on the biological binary nature of humanity. Even inanimate objects are given feminine and masculine attributions. In Arabic, "door" is masculine while "car" is feminine. Should these languages conform to English's gender neutrality or the new pronouns we're seeing? If so, how would that work? Should non-English languages abandon one of the genders and pick the other? If they pick the masculine instead of the feminine, would that send a signal to little girls that they aren't as important as boys? If they pick the feminine, does that tell boys something negative? And what about the poetry, prose, and other contributions of these languages? In poetry, artistic expressions may depend on the use of feminine or masculine word forms to rhyme or even make sense. This may seem easy for Western English speakers for whom there isn't a linguistic masculine/feminine distinction. But reconfiguring gender foists upon other cultures something they would find eviscer-ating. What could be more imperialistic than our society's autonomy dominating another's?

In the wake of the 2016 U.S. presidential election, former news anchor Dan Rather took to social media (particularly his public Facebook page) to decry what he perceived to be a one-sided ignoring of facts and science in a post-truth culture. Rather's comments are quite interesting, so I quote them at length:

> If people want to live in a post-truth world, where "elite" experts are all biased and facts are up for interpretation, I suggest they go all the way.
>
> You can go to a post-truth doctor who could say "well the elitist scientific tests say you have strep throat but I say it's cancer so let's give you some chemotherapy."
>
> Or you can go to a post-truth electrician who might say "well those elitist electrical manuals published in New York and those government regulations out of Washington say you should ground your electricity, but that's just a bunch of red tape."
>
> Or you can go to a post-truth auto mechanic who might say "well those elitist laws of physics say that this is how a braking system works, but let's replace your brake pads with fresh-baked chocolate chip cookies because they will smell better when you hit the brake pedal."
>
> The reality is that all of modern society, from the way your cell phone hooks up to your wi-fi, to the way the rain funnels into the storm drain, to the way your freezer keeps your ice cream frozen, is based on facts. It's because smart

people, who went to school and learned facts, collaborated to figure things out. And they wrote them down so that other people would know those facts and be able to build on them. That's how science works. That's how technology works. That's how modernity works.

Now that's not to say that there aren't things we don't understand, or things we have gotten wrong. But that's the great thing about facts and data. When they disprove something you thought, you can't—or at least shouldn't—ignore it. Once again, that's how progress happens.

The United States has risen to the most powerful and prosperous nation in human history based on facts, an educational system that taught them, a legal system that respected them, and a political system that made it all possible. That is the winning formula for the health and security of our nation, and the world. And if you don't like facts then I hope you don't ruin everything for those of us who do.

I find myself agreeing with much of this. But I wonder if Rather's analysis is too focused on the political sphere and only on one side, at that. He facetiously suggests that if we want to live in a post-truth world, we should "go all the way." I have news (pun intended) for Mr. Rather: We have done that. While we have yet to employ post-truth plumbers, we have employed post-truth professors, educated post-truth students, invested with post-truth bankers, sought guidance from post-truth clergy, listened to post-truth journalists, and elected post-truth politicians. In our Culture of Confusion, we've sacrificed the very clarity and reason Mr. Rather longs for on the altar of autonomy.

The Second Sacrifice: Our Moral Accountability

"Man is the measure of all things," Protagoras brashly proclaimed centuries ago. One would think that in the light of both ancient and contemporary history, we would be a little more circumspect about our magnificence today. But alas, we're more enamored with our educations, our sophistications, and ourselves. Tom Flynn, a prolific and thoughtful secular humanist writer, isn't more verbose than Protagoras, but makes essentially the same claim about humanity's ability to master itself and the world. "Through a process of value inquiry informed by scientific and reflective thought, men and women can reach *rough agreement concerning values,* crafting ethical systems that deliver optimal results for human beings in a broad spectrum of circumstances (emphasis mine).[10] We're in this thing together, Flynn would argue, and since there is no God to help us, we have to help ourselves. Our supposedly benign reflective thought and scientific inquiry will ultimately result in a "rough agreement" about moral values.

But underlying Flynn's optimism is the humanity-old striving for chaos-bound autonomy. It's but a hair's breadth away from secular humanism to self-worship and supreme authority. According to Jeremy Rifkin, "We no longer feel ourselves to be guests in someone else's home. . . . No set of pre-existing cosmic rules. . . . It is our creation now. We make the rules. We are responsible for nothing outside ourselves. We are the kingdom, and the power, and the glory."[11] Without enough of a pause or sober-minded reflection on whether self-glorification is wise, without sufficient reflection on humanity's pockmarked history of violence and ugliness, we flood the temples of *Deus Homo* with our worship.

Alexander Pope poetically laid bare the consequences of our self-deification in his *Essay on Man*:[12]

> Snatch from His hand the balance and the rod,
> Re-judge His justice, be the god of God.
> In pride, in reas'ning pride, our error lies;
> All quit their sphere, and rush in to the skies.
> Pride still is aiming at the blest abodes,
> Men would be angels, angels would be gods.
> Aspiring to be gods, if angels fell,
> Aspiring to be angels, men rebel:
> And who but wishes to invert the laws
> Of Order, sins against the Eternal Cause.

Indeed we have inverted the law's order. Anyone can do anything or be anyone. That's why moral confusion is the virtue of the day. We can cross the bounds of reality and justify it by this virtue. Moral clarity, on the other hand, shows us the objective truth beyond our preferences, the boundaries and limits to which we ought to conform. So clarity has become the vice of the day.

When humanity is the measure of all things, what isn't permissible anymore? It was Ivan, in Fyodor Dostoyevsky's *The Brothers Karamazov*, who said, "Without God . . . everything is permitted." We used to think that famous line was nothing more than an alarmist's overstatement. The reality is that Ivan didn't go far enough. When everything is permitted, autonomy can run amok. When autonomous self-sovereignties clash, reasonless power can be the only arbiter. Human autonomy is far more dangerous than animal autonomy. Where animals are semi-autonomous because there are no laws constricting them, they still have to follow their inherent instincts. But humans are different. We have the capacity to question and resist our baser drives. We can ask not just whether we *can* do something, but whether we *should* do something. That morality-based ability atrophies in a state of unchecked autonomy, where preferences matter more than truth. Autonomous animals obey instinct. Humans once obeyed truth. When animals collide in nature, power is what decides. But when human autonomies collide with no sense of accountability, the kind of power that can annihilate entire societies decides. Yet here we are now, in a world where practically anything is permissible except the idea that some things shouldn't be.

Now, I must be clear. Like true humanists, I have a high view of human nature. Unlike secular humanists, however, I believe that we are all made in the image of God—the *Imago Dei* (Gen. 1:27; 5:1)—and we have been created "a little lower than the heavenly beings and crowned . . . with glory and honor" (Psalm 8:5). But in our human rebellion against that purpose—in wanting to be God instead of being with God—we have become less than our intended and best selves. The paradox is that in striving to go from bearing the *Imago Dei* (with accountability to God) to *Deus Homo* (with accountability to no one), we have lost what it means to be human and to value other human beings.

The Third Sacrifice: Our Sense of Human Value

When we become laws unto ourselves and become the measure of all things, then we determine which humans are valuable and which ones are not. Certain philosophers with the highest academic credentials write with steady pens and argue with straight faces that certain *homo sapiens* simply aren't intrinsically valuable. Peter Singer espouses a utilitarian philosophy that says what is "good" is that which benefits the largest number of people, and what is "bad" is that which unnecessarily harms people. And yet Singer argues that human babies—*after they have been born*—can be killed by their parents.[13] Those babies, Singer argues, are not really persons because they lack the mental capacity to value themselves. The parents, on the other hand, have the capacity to assign value to the baby. So, if the parents don't value the baby or find that caring for the baby imposes a hardship on them, then the baby has no value and can be disposed of. Singer is on record as saying that a fetus or a baby with Down syndrome has no more value than that of a pig kept for livestock. Singer's conclusion is that "membership of the species Homo sapiens is not enough to confer a right to life."[14] He's not alone in his thinking. Two medical ethicists, Alberto Giubilini and Francesca Minerva, have advocated for a parent's right to kill a newborn baby born with infirmities if it would impose a hardship on the parents.[15]

Where does one even begin to respond to such ideas? In the Culture of Confusion fueled by our desire for autonomy, does anyone even have standing to object? Think of what Singer and his ilk are advocating. Parents have the autonomy to end a baby's life because they have the authority to determine whether the baby's value justifies the burden of caring for it. And if that burden impinges on the parents' autonomy, then the baby can be eliminated. This is the essence of unfettered human autonomy—to become as God but without the benefit of divine wisdom. We have become gods unaccountable to anyone or anything. David Bentley Hart points out that we "place ourselves not at the disposal of God, or the gods, or the Good, but before an abyss, over which presides the empty power of our isolated wills, whose decisions are their own moral index."[16]

In our confused quest to elevate ourselves to deities, we actually have become devils. We've commoditized the most vulnerable members of our species and consumed them as a kind of burnt offering to self-appeasement.

Here's where our atrophied reason and moral accountability intersect. Singer says we have no moral obligation to keep a baby with Down syndrome alive because we should limit the suffering and hardship of the parents.[17] And yet Singer argues that we have a moral obligation to help those victimized by poverty or famine because doing so serves the consequentialist ethic of benefiting the greatest number of people. When we choose to help others who are so afflicted, however, aren't we making ourselves uncomfortable, sometimes profoundly so? If we impose that obligation on others, aren't we forcing discomfort on them too? What's the difference between killing a baby that causes me discomfort and letting a suffering adult die for the same reason? Singer may respond that poverty-stricken people are true "persons" because they have the cognitive ability to value themselves. But that distinction is arbitrary. If cognitive ability is the marker for human value, then those who don't meet that arbitrary threshold would have no value. Less self-aware people would have less value. The less intelligent would have less value. Because cognitive awareness is notoriously difficult to measure, who would get to decide who has value and who doesn't? Again, we're back to the law of the jungle where animals eat the weak among their offspring. Only we don't eat them. We put them in a medical waste receptacle. The problem is that we are utterly unqualified for God's job:

> We are more powerful than ever before, but have very little idea of what to do with all that power. Worse still, humans seem to be more irresponsible than ever before. Self-made gods with only the laws of physics to keep us company, we are accountable to no one. We are consequently wreaking havoc on our fellow animals and on the surrounding ecosystem, seeking little more than our own comfort and amusement, yet never finding satisfaction.
>
> Is there anything more dangerous than dissatisfied and irresponsible gods who don't know what they want?[18]

The world seems to be spiraling out of control, and yet we cling to our idol of autonomy, relying on our own ingenuity to deliver us. Is it possible that we have become so confused that we mistake our decay as flourishing? Have we confused the odor of decomposition for the scent of a garden?

The Ironic Sacrifice: Losing Our Freedom in the Quest for Autonomy

When autonomy robs us of our reason, our accountability, and our value for individuals, we become desperate for deliverance from the chaos. But with our reason atrophied and our value for each other diminished, it will be easy for a charismatic and powerful individual, or perhaps a group of them, to start undermining some people's freedoms to serve other people's autonomy. That may sound farfetched, but it is already happening in our day.

On college campuses, the powers that be have revoked or attempted to revoke the approved status of Christian groups because they restricted their leadership (*not* membership) to Christians. In other words, they are being penalized for being Christian. In California, legislators passed a bill making it punishable by a fine for a long-term care facility or someone working there to "willfully and repeatedly fail to use a resident's [of the facility] preferred name or pronouns after being clearly informed of the preferred name or pronouns."[19] If someone is a biological male but asks you to call him a woman, the state will punish you if you refuse to do so. In other words, the state will take away your freedom if you fail to bow to someone else's autonomy.

It isn't just Christians or conservatives who feel the pressure. Richard Dawkins was disinvited from a Berkeley, California, radio station due to his critiques of Islam. University professors of every political bent are being attacked, shouted down, branded as racists for not succumbing to student sensibilities.[20] Confusing freedom with autonomy has enslaved our rational minds and our moral senses. And soon it may enslave us altogether.

Not So Out of Touch After All

This pursuit of autonomy drives increasingly ferocious attacks against the Bible as the standard for truth and conduct. Many oppose the Scriptures as an outmoded method of control that arbitrarily suppresses human behavior. This stems from the failure to see the differences between unfettered individual autonomy and true freedom. They are not the same. The Bible opposes the former and champions the latter. Lest we think the Bible is too outdated a document to lift us out of our contemporary mindset, let's consider some biblical examples that speak directly to our contemporary climate.

In the years after God had delivered them out of Egyptian slavery, the Hebrews had enjoyed a healthy freedom under the sovereignty of God. As Os Guinness says, it was a "consent of the governed." Sadly, it was only for a time. The Old Testament book of Judges tells us of Israel's rejection of freedom and quest for autonomy, a desire to have no authority above themselves. "In those days there was no king in Israel. Everyone did what was right in his own eyes" (Judges 17:6). In other words, they pursued preferences over truth. Each time the people's thirst for autonomy landed them in trouble, God sent a judge—a person who took his authority from God—to guide the people. But they rejected God's authority time and again in favor of their personal sovereignty until the resultant chaos became too much. Eventually, the people cried out for a human king (1 Samuel 8:4–6). As the Bible puts it, this was a rejection not of the judges and prophets who had guided Israel, but of God himself as the determiner of what is good and valuable (vv. 8–9).

It was disastrous. With limited exceptions, the successive kings were wicked despots, guided by their own autonomy. The people did not seek to root out bad leaders with truth, facts, and moral reasoning. Kings seized power through treachery, lies, and murder. It was chaos. Bad leaders were supplanted by equally, if not more, corrupt leaders because truth was no longer the arbiter of human conduct.

When we deal with our leaders today, whether we think they are good or bad or somewhere in the middle, do we do it with truth as our guide? Or do we proceed in the post-truth way, where we shred the truth a bit, and sometimes a lot, to get our person in office or get our agenda set? Such actions will lead to the same chaos that Israel experienced. To paraphrase Mark Twain, history won't repeat itself, but it will rhyme.

By no means do I intend to advocate for a theocracy in pointing out these parallels. In fact, I don't mean to get political at all. What I'm trying to point to are the cultural and moral consequences of jettisoning truth as our guide. We may end up with autonomy, but not freedom. What I am advocating for each one of us, individually in our hearts, is to search once again for the source of true freedom. It will be no surprise that I believe that God provides us with true freedoms that come from clarifying the confusion that has saturated the culture and blinded us from seeing who and what we were intended to be. Allow me in these concluding sentences to offer an observation that ties this chapter together.

The Gospel of John records an interesting exchange between Jesus and people who believed in him. Jesus says, "If you abide in my word, you are truly my disciples, and you will know the truth, and the truth will set you free" (John 8:31–32). The audience's reply is fascinating. "We are offspring of Abraham and have never been enslaved to anyone. How is it that you say, 'You will become free'?" (John 8:33). What a strange and confused response. How could they forget their four-hundred-year bondage in Egypt, the liberation from which they celebrated every Passover holiday for hundreds of years? And yet they did forget it. In fact, so confused was their thinking that they forgot that they were under Roman occupation at the very moment they claimed not to be enslaved to anyone. But they so valued their autonomy that they failed to see the truth of their enslavement right before their eyes. Autonomy is so distortive that self-evident truths are ignored to win an argument or to keep ourselves comfortable. We need to know the truth that our quest for autonomy is what enslaves us. We are in chains that we cannot feel and in prisons we cannot see. And they are both of our own making.

That is enough for the diagnosis of the problems that arise from confusion. It is time now for us to explore the solutions that come from clarity.

CHAPTER 4

Clarity about Freedom

History's most influential person expressly binds freedom to the limits of truth. "You will know the truth," Jesus says, "and the truth will set you free" (John 8:32). Jesus repudiates the post-truth Culture of Confusion's mindset that refuses to tether freedom to truth. Yet he does so without shaking his fist. He gently tells us that truth is freedom's foundation and the wall that protects freedom from the invasion of chaotic autonomy.

Jesus' exact wording expresses something subtle that we must not miss. He puts knowing the truth *first. Then* the truth will set us free. Today we have reversed things. In the West especially, we see freedom as the initial condition necessary to pursue truth. There is some intuitiveness to that, of course. We need academic freedom to explore and pursue scientific, philosophical, social, and religious truths. One of the best ways to learn how the world works is through the freedom to singe our fingers in the fire a little, to learn things the hard way, so to speak.

Our intuition that freedom precedes truth's discovery must be kept in proper focus, however. Freedom to pursue the truth comes only when we recognize that there is an objective truth out there for us to freely pursue. According to Jesus, truth and freedom are always linked. Any attempt to separate them diminishes our ability to enjoy either.

There's a cyclical nature to it all, isn't there? Our recognition that there are objective truths to be discovered leads to the freedom to discover them. In turn, our discoveries foster greater freedom to pursue yet more truths. The primer for starting this cycle in the first place is recognizing that there are objective truths that don't depend on the opinions or preferences we so highly exalt today. The truth-and-freedom cycle can be self-perpetuating once it gets going, unless something derails it. The post-truth Culture of Confusion does exactly that by throwing the monkey wrench of preferences in the works. How amazing that Jesus' two-thousand-year-old words should speak to us today, urging us to get the truth-and-freedom cycle back on track by putting things in their proper order.

Before we unpack how that can happen, let's think about one other pairing Jesus makes. Just a few moments after saying that the truth will set us free, Jesus makes the astonishing statement that if he—the Son—sets us free, we will be free indeed (John 8:36). In other words, Jesus claims to be the very truth that sets us free. Notice that he doesn't claim to *have* the truth that sets us free. He claims *to be* the truth that sets us free. That's quite the audacious statement, isn't it? Why believe him? We will find out why as we unpack just how applicable Jesus' words are to our current cultural confusion and our desperate need to clarify the nature of freedom.

Defining Freedom

If freedom is not synonymous with unfettered autonomy, then what does it mean? We use the word *freedom* so often and so glibly that its meaning has been taken for granted, if not lost altogether. Even when we understand that autonomy isn't identical to freedom, we still think of freedom one-dimensionally. In his excellent book *A Free People's Suicide*, social critic Os Guinness tells us that "freedom sounds simple, straightforward and self-evident. . . . But freedom is both more complex and more contested than many realize, so those who would guard freedom with care must regard freedom with respect."[1] In other words, to get clear on what it means to be free, we need to appreciate all of freedom's facets.

To help us, Guinness points to Isaiah Berlin's definitions of *negative freedom* and *positive freedom*. According to Berlin, negative freedom is the *"freedom from*—in essence, *freedom from* interference and constraint."[2] This is what we typically think of when we think of freedom. And that facet of freedom, on its own, dangerously resembles the sheer autonomy that leads to chaos. What's needed in addition to negative freedom is positive freedom, which is *"freedom for*—in essence, *freedom for* excellence according to whatever vision and ideals define that excellence."[3] Negative freedom and positive freedom go hand in hand. We need freedom from unnecessary restraints and interference so that we can exercise freedom for acting in the interests of the greater ideal. That ideal operates as a self-imposed restraint, keeping us from abusing our negative freedom. In other words, positive freedom is the ability to do not just what we *want*, but what we *should*. Objective moral truth is, therefore, critical to positive freedom and thus critical to freedom as a whole. That's why Jesus binds truth and freedom together.

Today's unbalanced idolization of negative freedom crosses ideological lines, muddling the thinking of liberals and conservatives alike. Again, Os Guinness is on point: "Today both American conservatives and liberals often speak as if negative freedom were all there is. . . . Liberals view freedom as freedom from the imposition of others . . . and conservatives as freedom from government encroachment."[4] This is so paradoxical because our emphasis on negative freedom deprives us of that which made Western civilization's societal triumphs so pioneering. Mere freedom from restraint doesn't encourage us to engage in the great quests to better society or to help others. Simply put, focusing on freedom from restraint encourages a sort of narcissistic preoccupation on the self and the fulfillment of our private desires. That kind of shallow freedom doesn't inspire us to do what is best for others or to act in the interests of the common good. We may think we are serving the common good when we champion the freedom of others to do whatever they want, but we're really just thinking inwardly, trying to prevent others from imposing restraints on what we want to do. In fact, it's gone further than that. In our obsession with negative freedom, we no longer want the ability *to do* whatever we want without restraint, we want the ability *to be* whatever we want without restraint.

A fully orbed view of freedom that equally embraces positive freedom—the freedom for the common good—will serve us better. History has shown this time and again. Whenever humanity has coupled our love of negative freedom to our need for positive freedom, tremendous public good has resulted. As Guinness says, from the banning of infanticide to the abolition of slavery to the civil rights movement, "none of the great liberal reforms of the West could have succeeded on the basis of negative freedom alone, and none will be launched on such a basis in the future."[5]

This must not be ignored. Positive freedom to pursue true ideals gave birth to the great movements that restored negative freedom to the disenfranchised and abused. Those triumphs were only the start. There is much more work to be done. The number of people trafficked in the sex trade is still in the millions, which means that we have yet to vanquish slavery. Ethnic and racial minorities still suffer discrimination, which means the civil rights movement cannot afford to rest. And unborn and post-born babies are still snuffed out for convenience's sake, which means we still don't value every person equally. If we fail to see the importance of our freedom to do what we should, none of the triumphs of the past can endure or make much-needed strides forward.

What's more, our one-sided glorification of freedom is the kind of thing that eventually can eat us alive individually. The late David Foster Wallace, a brilliant American writer, incisively pointed out that "there is actually no such thing as atheism," and all of us, regardless of our religious or non-religious bents, worship something. And if what we worship isn't transcendent but only based on a personal preference, our idol will eventually consume us. "If you worship money and things—if they are where you tap real meaning in life—then you will never have enough. Never feel you have enough.

It's the truth. Worship your own body and beauty and sexual allure and you will always feel ugly, and when time and age start showing, you will die a million deaths before they finally plant you. . . . Worship power—you will feel weak and afraid, and you will need ever more power over others to keep the fear at bay. Worship your intellect, being seen as smart—you will end up feeling stupid, a fraud, always on the verge of being found out. And so on."[6]

That's quite an observation from someone who, as far as I can tell, wasn't a religious believer. Overvaluing freedom from restraint qualifies for the same kind of idol worship that Wallace warns us about. If obsessions with transient things like appearance, wealth, success, and even our intellect have the potential to eat us alive, wouldn't the idolization of our right to do whatever we want pose the same danger? Worship beauty and we'll feel ugly. Worship power and we'll feel weak. Worship freedom from restraint and we'll feel enslaved, always hungering for more freedom and less restraint.

We can already see how our idol of negative freedom has begun to eat up our lives, can't we? We can engage in almost any sexual act we want with almost whomever we want, only to get shackled to medications or plagued by harmful relationships. We can indulge our visual appetites with uninhibited vigor, only to have our most cherished relationships destroyed because we're chained to our pornography-accessing screens. Technology has freed us to connect with people who live hemispheres away but has shrunk our worldview to just a few square inches of screen. We can freely imbibe in consciousness and conscience-altering substances, only to lock ourselves into rehab facilities.[7] How gruesomely ironic it is that our one-sided idolization of negative freedom has turned us into the land of the free and the home of the addicted.

It's easy to see how we got so focused on negative freedom. Think of all the movies whose central theme is freedom. From *Braveheart* to *The Patriot*, from *Saving Private Ryan* to *Amistad* and *Glory*, our stories focus on the human struggle to win (negative) freedom or to keep someone else from taking it away. These are true and good stories, ones we should tell ourselves over and over again. But it's interesting that we seldom see movies focused on what it takes to maintain freedom or to establish a system of government that properly orders it. That's because winning negative freedom presents a compelling story.

We spend so much time inventing new negative freedoms to win that we don't pause to think about what life should be like once we have them. The American founders thought of the end game—what we would and should do with our freedom of self-governance once we'd won it. John Adams powerfully wrote in his May 12, 1780, letter to Abigail Adams:

> I must study Politicks and War that my sons may have liberty to study Mathematicks and Philosophy. My sons ought to study Mathematicks and Philosophy, Geography, natural History, Naval Architecture, navigation, Commerce and Agriculture, in order to give their Children a right to study Painting, Poetry, Musick, Architecture, Statuary, Tapestry, and Porcelaine.[8]

The heroes of our freedom-winning films don't give rallying speeches about the crucial procedures necessary to sustain that freedom. And we certainly don't see sweeping sagas about

teaching ourselves what it means to have self-restraint for positive freedom (probably because such movies would be terribly
boring). But the effort to subdue our own passions and preferences and submit to the facts of reality and the moral truth of
what we ought to do is just as daunting and heroic. In fact, I'd
say it's even more heroic because it requires us to forsake the
glamour of limitless negative freedom.

Freedom Bound

Clarity about freedom comes only when we see its multiple facets. We need the negative freedom from unnecessary outside
restraints, but we also need boundaries and borders so that we
can be free for the greater good. To talk only of negative freedom is to talk about a one-sided coin. Single-sided freedom is
ultimately meaningless. The paradox we have to wrestle with
is that freedom, to be truly life-affirming, must be bound by
the moral restraint to act for the benefit of others as well as
ourselves. As Os Guinness puts it, "the only restraint that does
not contradict freedom is self-restraint."[9]

This is a major reason why the Bible is viewed with increas-
ing hostility in the West. The Culture of Confusion thinks
that the Bible stands against human freedom, with its seemingly arbitrary restraint on certain behaviors. And we tend to
view restraints on our freedoms, especially seemingly arbitrary
restraints, as immoral. We've come to think of freedom as if
it were a virtue in and of itself. We reverentially refer to the
"fight for freedom." Military operations are called "Operation
Enduring Freedom." And we erect a building in defiance of
terrorism and name it the "Freedom Tower." But freedom from

restraint isn't a virtue—it's a morally neutral state of being. After all, humans have freely performed tremendous acts of heroism and vile acts of atrocity.

Our veterans and honored dead did not make their sacrifices simply for our freedom from restraint (negative freedom). They also sacrificed for our freedom for the virtuous life (positive freedom). We often think that "it's good to be free" or "freedom is the greatest good." A clearer understanding of freedom allows us to act with the sacredness of other human beings in mind, and we can only be sacred beings if our value comes from God, the source who transcends human opinion. Positive freedom is linked to the sacredness of human beings, so it must be vigilantly guarded with boundaries if it is to endure and have meaning.

An illustration may help. My family enjoys the blessing of a big backyard, but that yard abuts a major road. Now, when our kids were younger, my wife and I set boundaries beyond which the kids could not go. Without those boundaries, we would have been worried that a ball might bounce into the road and kids, being inattentive as they are, might have chased that ball into traffic. The boundaries protected not only their safety but also their freedom. Without those boundaries, our kids wouldn't have had the freedom to enjoy the yard for its intended purpose.

Boundaries apply in every area of freedom, even in the arts where freedom of expression is often seen as totally unbound. In his inimitable way, G. K. Chesterton explains why: "The moment you step into the world of facts, you step into a world of limits. You can free things from alien or accidental laws, but not from the laws of their own nature. You may, if you like, free a tiger from his bars; but do not free him from his stripes. Do not free a camel of the burden of his hump: you may be freeing him from being a camel."[10]

If artistic freedom needs boundaries, how much more do other areas of freedom?

Think of what the Culture of Confusion's focus on autonomy has resulted in. We have given negative freedom a steroid-infused shot of adrenaline. We now want to be free from any restrictions on what we can *be*, not just what we can *do*. That isn't a real freedom if what we want to be doesn't line up with the reality of what we are. We may remove social boundaries, just as we might free a tiger from his cage. But we can no more free ourselves from our nature as humans, male or female, than we can a tiger from his stripes or a camel from his hump. If we barrel through the boundaries of what we are, we may free ourselves from what we were meant to be in the first place. The pursuit may be intoxicatingly liberating. For some it will feel like the ultimate achievement of self-deification. For others, it may seem like the answer to a lifelong struggle with self-identification. But if the statistics are to be taken at all seriously, the hard reality is that for most people, unbounded freedom results in emotional and spiritual enslavement. Reality is full of limitations. No amount of desire or drive can alter that reality or remove those boundaries.

Contrary to contemporary belief, the Bible doesn't set up arbitrary boundaries to oppose our freedom. Its boundaries favor our fulfillment. The Bible, in which God tells each of us about our uniqueness and value, stands against the stealthy enslavement that comes from a muddled, one-sided view of freedom. We can see this in the very structure of the New Testament itself. The four gospels chronicle Jesus' glorious winning of our freedom over sin through his life, death, and resurrection. That's why the vast majority of movies based on the New Testament focus on the four gospel narratives. But the New Testament also gives us the book of Acts, where the disciples wrestle with what it means to have had the Old Testament law and yet enjoy the freedom that comes through Jesus' fulfillment of that law. With the guidance of the Holy Spirit, the disciples debate and discover how to live for the greater good *after* Jesus had won their spiritual freedom.

We also have the New Testament's doctrinal books. From the writings of Paul, Peter, James, Jude, John, and others we learn how our spiritual freedom ought to be put into practice and how that freedom can be sustained without devolving into bedlam. The process of winning freedom as told in the Gospels is the foundation, but the understanding of what to do with that freedom and what limits it might have on our ethics and behavior are given just as much focus in the New Testament. In its very structure, the Bible describes freedom in all its aspects, from winning it to structuring it to maintaining it. Only the Lord of history, the Lord of language, can craft something whose very organization speaks as powerfully as the words it contains. God knows us through and through. He knows that it is in our nature to focus too narrowly and to go too far even with things he has blessed us with. David Foster Wallace's previously mentioned warning that what we worship will eventually eat us is insightful, but it's not new. He actually echoes the millennia-old words of Paul:

> For you were called to freedom, brothers. Only do not use your freedom as an opportunity for the flesh, but through love serve one another. For the whole law is fulfilled in one word: "You shall love your neighbor as yourself." But if you bite and devour one another, watch out that you are not consumed by one another. (Galatians 5:13–15)

The wisdom of holy writ shows itself again. Paul tells us about the need to self-restrain our negative freedom so that we can act in each other's best interests, which is positive freedom. If we don't, if we worship freedom in the service of self-gratification, we'll end up devouring each other. How remarkable it is that God, knowing us, has established the boundaries of freedom that keep us from running blindly into traffic, childishly chasing after the bouncing ball of our liberty.

Freedom's Foundation in God

Freedom becomes clear when we recognize that God is freedom's unchanging source. America's founding was a daring attempt to institute a government that acknowledged and encouraged both negative freedom and positive freedom. The Declaration of Independence tells us that every person has inalienable rights to life, liberty, and the pursuit of happiness. The key word is *inalienable.* By definition, a right is inalienable because no person or group of people (like the government or society) can take it away. When someone is enslaved, her right to liberty isn't taken away even though it is violated. After I made that statement during a public debate on the nature of rights, my opponent accused me of playing a semantic game. But surely it's not a matter of mere semantics. If slavery took away a person's right to be free, that right would be gone and therefore her continued slavery wouldn't be immoral. Regimes that have rejected God and viewed freedom as a creation of the state have historically oppressed human freedom and rights—from Stalinist Russia to nationally socialist Germany, from communist China to Kim Jong-Un's North Korea. Inalienable rights, therefore, must be grounded in a source beyond human authority. In this way, their existence doesn't depend on human opinion, reasoning, or behavior. If they did, inalienable rights simply wouldn't exist. And if inalienable rights don't exist, then America itself is an illusion. As we'll see very shortly, even those among us with allegiance to atheistic naturalism agree that without God, freedom itself is an illusion.

The Declaration of Independence's drafters understood this well. The Declaration states that in rebellion against monarchical tyranny, the colonists would "assume among the powers of the earth the separate and equal station to which the Laws of Nature and of Nature's God entitle them." But reliance on a mere (though important) document like the Declaration of Independence or the U.S. Constitution isn't enough. Those are just the centuries-old statements of men in powdered wigs, after all. A declaration based merely on human preferences scrawled in pen across parchment is just as flimsy. But if it's founded on something—better yet *someone*—that transcends time, space, matter, and opinions, then the rights and freedoms it declares have transcendent substance. A simple syllogism may help us here:

1. The inalienable right to freedom exists only if God exists;
2. The inalienable right to freedom exists;
3. Therefore God exists.

What's fascinating is that brilliant atheistic thinkers agree with the thrust of this argument. For example, the famed Canadian atheist and philosopher Kai Nielsen writes, "Pure practical reason, even with a good knowledge of the facts, will not take you to morality."[11] While Nielsen doesn't specifically mention rights, his reflection is fitting because rights, including the right to liberty, are moral categories. As such, they exist in an objective sense only if they have their foundation in God.

Now in one sense, an atheist can agree with the Declaration that "We are endowed by our Creator with certain inalienable rights" if by *creator* the atheist means "unguided genetic mutations influenced by unguided natural selection." But with that kind of creator, the heart of the Declaration breaks down, doesn't it? We'd have to anthropomorphize evolution to have it endow us with anything. And what would evolution endow us with, exactly? Inalienable rights? How do we have rights if nature is red in tooth and claw, mindless of the morality of mass extinctions and—as atheist Richard Dawkins says—is blind, pitiless, and indifferent?[12] Indeed, fellow atheists Raymond Tallis and Thomas Nagel admit that unguided evolution can't even endow us with conscious power.[13] How then can we give ourselves rights? Without God, the right to liberty is simply vaporous.

But the problem goes even deeper if naturalism is true. If we're just complex chemical machines, then how do we actually have freedom, whether negative or positive? We don't make real choices; we just react to external stimuli based on our chemistry. That would mean we have no responsibilities, no rights, and no real freedom. A growing number of atheism's most influential voices, including that of popular author Sam Harris, acknowledge that human free will is an illusion if there is no God.[14]

If we have no free will—if our "brains made us do it"—we can't be praised for our heroism nor blamed for our cowardice. The implications are both fascinating and frightening. The frightening part is that studies have shown that people who believe they don't have free will are more likely to cheat on tests and lie. They are less likely to volunteer for socially responsible causes or give to aid the poor. In other words, "In every regard, it seems, when we embrace determinism, we indulge our dark side."[15] The fascinating part is that if failing to believe in free will leads to indulging our darker sides, then perhaps we do have free will after all.

Consider this: Why would we resort to less moral behaviors once we abandon belief in free will? Why would our brain chemistry suddenly revert to selfish and less socially responsible behavior if we fail to believe in moral accountability? Why don't we suddenly become more socially responsible instead of less? A naturalist might say that evolution is all about DNA propagation, which leads us to act selfishly. But that same naturalist also would argue that we are socially responsible animals because evolution has driven us to protect ourselves and ensure our survival through self-nurturing groups. Well, which is it? Might it be instead that we have a sinful nature and that in accordance with that sinful nature we choose to act immorally if we think that we won't be held accountable? We use our freedom to deny that free will exists so we can absolve ourselves of our selfishness. Might it be that Jesus was right when he said that the human heart is in desperate need of redemption from outside itself?[16]

There is a balance here. Our sinful nature and our physical nature influence our behaviors, but we also choose to act in submission or rebellion to those natures based on our beliefs about the world. That much is evident in the fact that we act more or less morally depending on whether we think we have free will. Our volition is only strong enough to overcome our sinful nature and physically driven desires temporarily, however, which makes a human-invented freedom so fragile. I think of a scene from the Oscar-winning film *Gladiator*. Just before the Roman Caesar Marcus Aurelius charges his top general with the responsibility of making Rome into a republic, Aurelius explains that Rome was originally intended to be a place where freedom was the ideal. "There was once a dream that was Rome," he says. "You could only whisper it. Anything more than a whisper and it would vanish, it was so fragile." Such is the fragility of our freedom in the West. Our godless understanding of freedom, as one-sided as it is, is so fragile that speaking of it any louder than a whisper will cause it to dissipate like smoke. In fact, if the contemporary mob rule that shouts down and violently attacks others for having out-of-fashion viewpoints is any indication, all we may be left with is whispering in hushed corners.

At some level, the religious and irreligious alike recognize how freedom *ought* to work. The Secular Humanist Declaration of 1980 recognizes that free inquiry requires securing freedoms of the press, association, philosophy, science, and religion. In fact, the Secular Humanist Declaration says that "free inquiry requires that we tolerate diversity of opinion and that we respect the right of individuals to express their beliefs, however unpopular they may be, without social or legal prohibition or fear of sanctions."[17] As much as I can agree with this statement, I can't help but notice that without God as its foundation, the sentiments it expresses are mere smoky vapors that vanish with anything more than a whisper. Because God exists, however, we have accountability beyond ourselves, making the sentiments concrete.

We have the right to freedom from human tyranny and freedom for the greater good—even for those with whom we disagree—because we have objective moral obligations, to God first and then to each other. As culture jettisons God, it manipulates our freedom from restraints into a freedom from criticism and discomfort. We can no longer tolerate being offended, so we have no obligation to afford freedom to someone who offends us. This has affected everyone, whether right or left, religious or secular. After being disinvited from appearing on a public radio station in Berkeley, California, because of his harsh criticisms of Islam, Richard Dawkins noted the hypocrisy of allowing him to freely criticize Christianity to thunderous applause on college campuses, only to have that freedom restricted because he had criticized a minority religion. Paul's words from Galatians that I referenced above have indeed come true in our day. We've used our freedom to bite and devour one another (Galatians 5:13–15).

This is why Tom Flynn's starry-eyed optimism that we'll reach "rough agreement" concerning values without God's help remains nothing more than a romantic notion. The post-truth Culture of Confusion has even turned on the secularists who told us that "man is the measure of all things." Despite our technological achievements and scientific inquiries, we haven't become as reflective as Flynn would like. Too often we've figured out new, better, and more sanitized ways to degrade each other—think of social media and cyberbullying—or to forcibly silence others because of their views. As we've become more autonomous, we've sought power to enforce our autonomy. We haven't come to Flynn's "rough agreement concerning values." We've just agreed to be rough.

This is not a new development. It was described 2,000 years ago in the pages of the Bible and on the lips of Jesus. Humanity, unbound by accountability to the divine, cannot be the source of fully realized freedom. But that doesn't mean there isn't a source.

Clarity about Freedom, Found in a Person

With a clearer, fuller view of freedom, let's revisit Jesus' words in John 8. Both negative freedom and positive freedom must be exercised within the boundaries of the truth. Our negative freedom from restraint must be bound by the truth that unfettered autonomy leads to chaos. Our positive freedom—our freedom for the greater good—must be bound by the truth that we can't forcibly coerce a good conscience into someone. Jesus is right when he tells us that the truth will set us free.

But there is still a greater depth in his words, something we've already alluded to but not yet fully explored. Jesus doesn't tell us that an abstract concept like "the truth" will set us free. He makes the truth tangible, even personal. He tells us that he, the Son, will set us free. It's at once an audacious and a powerful statement. Jesus' audience of Jews, children of Abraham, denies that they've ever been enslaved, so they don't need to be set free. Ignoring their failure to remember four hundred years of Egyptian bondage and the current Roman occupation, Jesus launches directly into what has truly—and most pervasively—enslaved humanity. "Truly, truly, I say to you, everyone who practices sin is a slave to sin. The slave does not remain in the house forever; the son remains forever. So if the Son sets you free, you will be free indeed" (John 8:34–36). Jesus can free us from the bondage of sin because he has no sins of his own from which he needs liberation. In other words, Jesus claimed to be the most free being in existence. Only God in the flesh, the source of all truth and freedom, can back up such a claim.

And back it up he did by raising himself from the dead. While space doesn't permit a detailed discussion of the remarkable evidence for the historical fact of Jesus' resurrection, suffice it to say that a number of excellent books have been written on the subject.[18] Summarizing much of that evidence at Western Michigan University, I debated the widely read atheist John Loftus on the evidence for Jesus' resurrection.[19] Jesus' resurrection gives us the ultimate reason to trust him. The religious leaders asked him to substantiate his claims of authority. He responded by saying that after they would destroy his body, Jesus would raise it up again three days later (John 2:18–19). That would be either true or false. It wouldn't be a matter of opinion. Jesus could have escaped factual scrutiny by claiming that he would rise in some esoteric way or that his message would live on. Jesus didn't have to give a specific (and therefore falsifiable) time frame in which he would bodily rise. But Jesus wasn't interested in playing to his hearers' preferences or fooling them into belief. He was interested in facts. And the fact is that the tomb in which he was buried was empty three days later because his body was no longer dead. The earliest Christian creeds—dating to just several years and possibly even just several months after the crucifixion—tell us of the eyewitness accounts of Jesus showing himself alive to hundreds of disciples. Those disciples were willing to die or did in fact die rather than recant their claim to have encountered the risen Christ. I've often been asked why I put my trust in Jesus when so many others have claimed to have the answers to life's big questions. My answer is always the same:

Jesus rose from the dead, and someone who rises from the dead has credibility.

That's what makes the gospel unique among religious and nonreligious messages claiming to offer us freedom. The gospel is rooted not in ideologies or ideas, but in identity—specifically Jesus' identity. He claimed to be the one who had no sin of his own and that he could therefore pay the price wrought by our sins. That price is separation from God, who intended us to have relationship with him. We only need to accept Jesus' payment on our behalf to be free from the sins that hold us back from that true purpose. That's what it means to be "free indeed." Os Guinness and others have taught us that true freedom is multifaceted. It includes negative freedom and positive freedom. We need *freedom from* restraint and *freedom for* the greater good.

May I add one more facet to "freedom indeed"? It's the

freedom from our sins and the consequences they bring. We were intended for relationship with God. That's why we human beings crave, covet, protect, and mourn the loss of relationships. We lost that relationship with God through the post-truth mentality of our first parents. Our sin separated us from that relationship, but Christ has come to restore it to us so that we can once again be what we were meant to be. And so freedom from sin is the added facet that's needed for "freedom indeed." Freedom from unnecessary restraint allows us to search out life's purpose and meaning. Freedom for the greater good adds moral virtue to truth seeking. And freedom from sin allows us to see who we really are. It's as straightforward as an equation, really, and it goes like this: Freedom from restraint + Freedom for the greater good + Freedom from sin = Freedom indeed to be what we were meant to be.

This is the essence of true freedom, and it doesn't depend on our circumstances or what any government gives or takes away. Mary Poplin, a former atheist, profoundly contrasts the shallow freedom she once sought absent God with the profound freedom she found in Christ. In fact, looking back she sees that the shallow freedom wasn't freedom at all. "The paradox was that when I thought I was most free, responsible and reasonable, I was least. I was a slave to my own desires and to the spirits that drove them. *Real freedom is something altogether different—it starts on the inside.* As martyrs and the persecuted have testified, we can have real freedom inside a prison wall."[20]

We either have an inherent dignity, a dignity that comes from the fact of our being human, or an incidental dignity, a dignity that comes from circumstances and the vicissitudes of human opinion. The kind of freedom Poplin found solidifies the inherent dignity of human beings. Our preferences about who and what we are, and our opinions about the value of other people, will ebb and flow. But if our dignity comes from a source outside ourselves, then it is truly inalienable. In that we are free. In that truth we have dignity. The confusion about who and what we are can find clarity. And it is the clarity about human dignity we will turn to next.

CHAPTER 5

Clarity about Human Dignity

It's at once an eye-catching and heart-warming piece of art. At the United Nations headquarters in New York is a stone mosaic based on a painting by the famous American artist Norman Rockwell. With Rockwell's characteristic detail and soft tones, the mosaic depicts people from different ethnic, racial, and religious backgrounds standing in solidarity. Inscribed in it are the words, "Do unto Others As You Would Have Them Do unto You." Inset into the beautiful visual art are the artful words that have come to be known worldwide as the Golden Rule. The mosaic has become one of the U.N. headquarters' most popular attractions.

The Golden Rule mosaic had cracked and deteriorated over time, needing restoration. How strangely poetic. As our culture's moral framework has crumbled, our understanding of the essence of human dignity has likewise cracked.

The restored *Golden Rule* mosaic was unveiled at a rededication ceremony during which U.N. Deputy Secretary-General Jan Eliasson explained its importance. "It reflects the very essence of our mission as set out in our Charter," he said. "At its core, the work is about narrowing the gap between the world as it is and the world as we want it to be."[1] Eliasson wasn't suggesting that the U.N.'s function is to fashion and create a world as humanity sees fit. I think he was saying that the U.N.'s work, at least in intention, is to narrow the gap between the fractured, violent world we see and the peaceful, human-dignifying world we wish we lived in. It's a noble sentiment, the realization of which has eluded us from time immemorial. In the Culture of Confusion where nothing seems anchored and uncertainty is lauded as virtue, we have to ask ourselves if we have any way to get back on track toward restoring a clear vision for the common good. Or will the fissures of confusion and uncertainty cause the mosaic of our hopes to further crumble?

The Golden Rule as inscribed on the U.N. mosaic is easily one of the most quoted and recognized idioms in human history. Yet we seldom realize who first uttered those words in that particular way. It was, of course, Jesus of Nazareth who said, "So in everything, *do to others what you would have them do to you,* for this sums up the Law and the Prophets" (Matthew 7:12 NIV, emphasis mine). This sentiment is also expressed in other religious and nonreligious traditions. In fact, the North American Interfaith Network gifted to the United Nations a poster also entitled "The Golden Rule," bearing its many versions. Among others, the poster displays versions from:

1. Hinduism: "This is the sum of duty: do not do to others what would cause pain if done to you" (Mahabharata 5:1517);
2. Buddhism: "Treat not others in ways that you yourself would find hurtful" (Udana-Varga 5.18);

3. Islam: "Not one of you truly believes until you wish for others what you wish for yourself" (Hadith); and

4. Unitarian Humanism: "We affirm and promote respect for the interdependent web of all existence of which we are a part."

Though subtle, there are important differences between Jesus' wording and the wordings in other traditions. We'll get to those later. But for now, it's important to see that all these versions express the common belief that we should demonstrate the value and dignity of other humans by our actions.

And yet we've veered far from that common belief, haven't we? Our social and political commentaries have gone from being polarized to *Hitlerized* as we indulgently use the word *hate* to describe anyone who doesn't agree with our views. Our common understanding of human dignity has fractured. We've become tribal. Those with whom we agree have dignity; everyone else is a hate-filled adversary. We've forgotten that we need each other to fit into a unified, designed mosaic.

Astonishingly, this all happened in an age of unprecedented information flow and connectivity. As we hurl ourselves headlong into a future of artificially boosted brains, chemically enhanced bodies, and culturally modified terms, we've lost sight of the fundamental definition of what it means to be human. We no longer pause to reflect on our basic foundations. Why not? Perhaps because pausing is impractical and slows us down. Nor does it yield easy-to-read pie charts or distraction-causing gadgets. Deep reflection amounts to nothing more than navel-gazing, or so our current thinking goes.

The truth is that our obsessions with technology, our own

genius, and our ability to self-define are the real navel-gazing. As we lose our grip on what it means to be human with inherent dignity, uncertainty and confusion take over. Technological, sexual, gender-based, and bio-tech questions have brought about what French philosopher Dominique Janicaud called "unprecedented uncertainty about human identity."[2] And if we have unprecedented uncertainty about our identity, how can we hope to have any sense of common dignity that impels us to do unto others as we would have done to us? We need a return to clarity about human dignity if we are to bridge the gap between the way the world is and the way we want it to be. Pausing and reflecting on our humanity is practical and progressive after all.

Fundamental questions need re-answering. Do we have free will or are we just chemical machines? Are humans special in some way apart from other animals? If we're not special, do we have anything like a sacred value? How can we justify our moral outrage at bigotry, racism, and the like if what it means to be human is a matter only of molecules in motion? It's difficult to answer these questions even when we do take the time to thoughtfully reflect.

I'm reminded of Supreme Court Justice Anthony Kennedy's famous statement (or infamous—opinions vary) that "At the heart of liberty is the right to define one's own concept of existence, of meaning, of the universe, and of the mystery of human life."[3] Surely that can't be correct. That kind of self-definition is at the heart of autonomy, not liberty. We don't have the intellectual foundation from which to ask basic questions about human dignity if an essential part of each person's liberty is to decide what they are and what other people are. To be fair, Justice Kennedy's next sentence reads, "Beliefs about these matters could not define the attributes of personhood were they formed under compulsion of the State." He meant to advocate for freedom from government intrusion into personal decisions. But his words go well beyond that and imply that individual human beliefs determine and define reality, including personhood. His statement could be the Culture of Confusion's creed. Every individual person can define existence, the universe, and human life.

In later Supreme Court decisions, Justice Kennedy has taken this principle of self-definition and applied it to human dignity. Most notably, he wrote the court's majority opinion striking down voter-ratified constitutional amendments in six states defining marriage as between one man and one woman.[4] It's ironic that according to Justice Kennedy, the majority voters in those states did *not* have the liberty to define their own concept of existence, meaning, the universe, and the mystery of life. But Justice Kennedy, an agent of the state, had the right and power to do it for them. In his decision, Justice Kennedy used the term *dignity* nine times. But what did he mean? Reading his opinion reveals little except, apparently, that we have dignity only if everything about us is celebrated. It's my firm belief that everyone, regardless of beliefs, orientations, and preferences, has inherent dignity and intrinsic value. But can I respect that dignity only if I affirm everything about another person? Or is it the case that acknowledging and respecting another person's dignity springs from something far deeper than human opinion?

Pushing Reset: Does Being
Human Really Mean Anything?

By and large, secular humanists don't believe in God, but many do affirm the objectivity of human value and dignity. Paul Kurtz, the author of the Secular Humanist Manifesto 2000, wrote that "the underlying ethical principle of Planetary Humanism is the need to respect the dignity and worth of all persons in the world community."[5] This sentence is substantively consistent with the Judeo-Christian ethic that all humans deserve respect and dignity. And so the first thing we should note is the common desire among the religious and nonreligious to affirm human dignity.

Yet at the heart of secular attempts to affirm objective human dignity lies a confused incoherence. According to the Humanist Manifestos I and II, "Ethics is autonomous and situational, needing no theological or ideological sanction." That statement is itself an ideology, which makes it self-defeating. They further state, "Human life has meaning because *we create and develop* our futures."[6] Similarly, the European Constitution recognizes that humans have value and dignity but doesn't ground them in a transcendent being like God. Instead, our value is derivative and developed: "Drawing inspiration from the cultural, religious and humanist inheritance of Europe, *from which have developed* the universal values of the inviolable and inalienable rights of the human person, freedom, democracy, equality and the rule of law."[7] In my previous book, *Grand Central Question*, I addressed this incoherence in greater detail.[8] Here, I just want to ask the question: How can human dignity and meaning be objectively true irrespective of human preference if *we* create and develop them? If Europeans "developed" universal values, then they aren't universal. To vaunt human autonomy, we have to say humans have inherent dignity. But for humans to have objective dignity, we can't be the autonomous definers of dignity. Here's the rub: The autonomy that we claim gives us dignity is the very autonomy that undermines it. That's as confused as things get.

There is a growing recognition of this confusion among secular thinkers, and some are unflinchingly trying to clarify matters by either explicitly or implicitly denying that humans have objective value and dignity. According to such voices, we are either just chemically sophisticated machines or evolutionarily gifted animals. But such views raise more problems than they solve.

We Are Just Sophisticated Machines. Philosophers and neuroscientists like Daniel Dennett and Sam Harris espouse the view that human beings, like all other creatures, are merely complex chemical machines that react to external stimuli. According to Dennett, we can explain the human mind the same way we explain every physical phenomenon, from radioactivity to photosynthesis.[9] Our consciousness is explained not by an immaterial soul but by our neurons and brain chemistries. We are, quite literally, our brains. We have no immaterial soul. There is nothing more to us than chemistry and physics. Thus, there is no objective purpose to humanity.

Things get worse for us when we take that mechanistic thinking and consider our place in the universe. Cosmically speaking, "we're just a bit of pollution," according to physicist Lawrence Krauss. "If you got rid of us . . . then the universe would be largely the same. We're completely irrelevant."[10]

Dousing the warm fuzzies with more ice water, Peter Atkins says of humanity that "gone is purpose; all that is left is direction. This is the bleakness we have to accept as we peer deeply and dispassionately into the heart of the universe."[11]

We Are Just Sophisticated Animals. Others put us just a step above universal flotsam, asserting that we are the unwitting recipients of directionless evolutionary advantages over other beasts. Through random genetic mutations and unguided natural selection, our species happens to be the most intelligent. Because our DNA functions solely to propagate itself, it has tricked us into developing moral notions of human dignity and value that prevent others from killing us. Atheist philosopher Michael Ruse makes the point that morality is nothing but an illusion foisted on us by our genes to get us to be social cooperators. Other than that illusion, nothing prevents us from acting like pagan Romans.[12]

So being sophisticated animals doesn't afford us any more dignity than being cosmic pollution. Dennett says that our evolutionary animality "eats through just about every traditional concept and dissolves the illusion of our own authorship, our own divine spark of creativity and understanding."[13] And John Gray unflinchingly tells us that all talk of human dignity is illusory. "Looking for meaning in history," he writes, "is like looking for patterns in could. Nietzsche knew this, but he could not accept it. He was trapped in the chalk circle of Christian hopes."[14]

The bars of a theoretical cage will not contain the consequences of believing that we are merely chemical machines or sophisticated animals. Those consequences roam wildly into the professions that affect our lives. I think of legal opinions written by Judge Richard Posner of the United States Court of Appeals for the Seventh Circuit. Posner was so influential that his opinions were required reading in law school across multiple areas of study. In an interview I recently came across, this famous jurist summed up his judicial philosophy this way: "People are monkeys with large brains. Period."[15] That struck me because it seems to contradict the very basis of the judicial system he served. If we are just monkeys with big brains, how can Judge Posner—or any judge for that matter—think that he joins other jurists whose noble calling is to impartially and thoughtfully adjudicate the affairs of free people? If Posner is right that we're just big-brained primates, how is he anything but a zookeeper whose job is just to keep the animals from biting each other? As our institutions of higher learning embrace a philosophy that reduces us to meat computers or gifted animals, all of their fields of study lose meaning. All notions of sacred callings and noble professions must go out the window.

Some time ago my wife, Nicole, and I were having dinner with a very successful doctor who was also an atheist. Nicole asked him a great question: "What gets you out of bed in the morning? What inspires you to do what you do?" His reply came quickly. "Helping people," he said magnanimously. "Other people are my purpose." I couldn't help but seize the opportunity for a follow-up question. "Why?" I asked. "Why do you find helping other people motivating?"

He looked at me as if I'd asked him quite possibly the silliest question in history. "What do you mean why? Because they're people." It seemed a fair enough response, but I was getting at the basis for his belief that human beings have any objective value that could possibly inspire him. So I had another follow-up question.

"I guess what I'm getting at is this: If you think we're just sophisticated chemical machines, then what makes you a doctor instead of just an expensively educated mechanic?" We had touched a special nerve in him. He had given so much of his time and money toward helping people get medical care, yet he had never given any serious thought to whether those people had any value at all. A deep and meaningful conversation followed.

Two things really are at play here. If human beings are reduced to machines or animals, there really is no nobility to anything we do because the recipients of our seemingly noble acts aren't really noble either. And yet, we can't seem to help thinking that we do have intrinsic dignity and that our professional pursuits are noble. Paul Kalinithi, a gifted young neurosurgeon, described the ever-present tug of seeing people as more than organic machines even as he was learning how to dissect the human body in his anatomy labs. Medical students tried to ignore the humanity of the cadavers by covering their faces or making jokes. But, as Kalinithi says, "In our rare reflective moments, we were all silently apologizing to our cadavers, not because we sensed the transgression but because we did not."[16] That tug is what discomfited the brilliant doctor we had dinner with that night. That tug is what infuses our legal opinions with references to *dignity* and *fairness*. These ideas, if they are to have any lasting and real meaning, cannot be divorced from a theistic framework that gives them substance.

Some secularists recognize the implications of the reductionist view and want to steer away from it. Peter Singer embraces the idea that we are just apes with better software. And so he asks, "Why should we believe that the mere fact that a being is a member of the species Homo Sapiens endows its life with some unique, almost infinite value?"[17] Singer's last question actually has an answer. We will get to it soon enough.

In this kind of thinking, our sacredness and dignity are no longer givens of the human condition, but products of mere preference. Sam Harris thinks that abandoning the illusion of free will in favor of deterministic neurochemistry is actually a good thing. Blaming our chemistry for our bad actions will free us (pun intended) from moral responsibility and so we won't hate people who do bad things. Instead, we'll understand that the malefactors don't need punishment. They need chemical enhancement.[18]

A number of questions spring up from this kind of thinking. First, where does it all end? If chemical determinism is true, we may be chemically predisposed to hate people who do bad things because of their chemistry. Must the haters be chemically treated too? Second, notice the inherent contradiction. Harris and Dennett arrived at their conclusions that we don't have free will, supposedly by drawing conclusions from the available evidence. But, assuming they are not superhuman, weren't Dennett and Harris chemically destined to come to those conclusions? Their chemistries led them to believe that we have no free will while my chemistry leads me to believe that we do. Their reactions could be true or false and neither they, nor we, have any way to know which. According to the determinism of Dennett and Harris, even as you read these words, the assessments you're making about the value of my arguments aren't *rational* reactions—they're just *chemical* reactions. Ironically, Sam Harris didn't freely choose to write his book *Free Will*.

The reality is that not only is strict determinism philosophically untenable, it's also scientifically unprovable. Raymond Tallis, an atheist neurologist, picks apart the various brain scans and psychological studies that attempt to prove we are nothing more than brain chemistry.[19] In fact, quite the opposite is true. An impressive body of scientific evidence demonstrates that the mind is not the brain and that human mental activity survives brain death.[20] While no friend to theism, Tallis acerbically critiques today's fashionable reductionism: "Neuroscientists who think they have found the circuits in a brain corresponding to wisdom seem to lack that very quality, as a result of which they are oblivious even to what the more critical minds in their own discipline are saying."[21]

Tallis's candor and willingness to call out his colleagues' overeager reductionism sometimes makes his arguments look theistic. He convincingly refutes Dennett's argument that human intentionality is nothing more than the kind of software we might see in a robot. Specifically, Tallis points out Dennett's failure to recognize that the robot's software was *intentionally* written by humans.[22] He says that a robot's intentionality is the product of design. That is exactly what a Christian would say. Our human intentionality is not a naturally occurring phenomenon. It is something put into us by a designer. Tallis's brilliant critique of his fellow atheists practically puts him on the church steps.

Some naturalists argue that humans are nothing more than computers or animals. Other atheists argue that human consciousness transcends the physical, yet God can't be the explanation. Is it any wonder that confusion about what it means to be human and what it means to have dignity abound?

Strangely, one of the Bible's chief figures, Solomon, asked the same questions that contemporary secularists ask:

> I said in my heart with regard to the children of man that God is testing them that they may see that they themselves are but beasts. For what happens to the children of man and what happens to the beasts is the same; as one dies, so dies the other. They all have the same breath, and man has no advantage over the beasts, for all is vanity. All go to one place. All are from the dust, and to dust all return. Who knows whether the spirit of man goes upward and the spirit of the beast goes down into the earth? So I saw that there is nothing better than that a man should rejoice in his work, for that is his lot. Who can bring him to see what will be after him? (Ecclesiastes 3:18–22)

If we're nothing more than animals or chemical machines, then we can never arrive at true *answers* to Solomon's questions, only chemically determined, stimulus-motivated *responses*. But Solomon asked his questions from within a theistic framework. Paradoxically, this means that Solomon can exercise his God-given rationality and consciousness to arrive at an answer.

This is exactly what Tallis struggles with. He rejects any notion of supernaturalism, calling it a prison. Yet he laments that strict naturalism leads to the kind of thinking that lessens our dignity as human beings. As a neurologist, he sees the empirical and philosophical bankruptcy of the effort to reduce humans to chemical machines because neither neuroscience (something he practices) nor Darwinian evolution (an idea he espouses) can explain why human beings possess a form of consciousness that is so qualitatively different from that of any other animals. We must continue to ask what it means to be human because we can't afford not to. "If any ideas are important," Tallis writes, "then ideas about the kind of creatures we are must be of supreme importance."[23]

Indeed, the idea of what we are, and whether we have any dignity at all, is of supreme importance. Otherwise, the morass of contradictory confusion will continue to paralyze us. Through unfettered autonomy, we make ourselves into gods who are accountable to no one. And then we use our divinity to declare that we are less than human. Perhaps confusion is too mild a word to describe our culture.

Secular Confusion: We Are Equal to God, but Less than Human

Sometimes these contradictory views collide right before our eyes. Recently, I watched a video of Princeton University professor Liz Harmon explaining her ethics of early-stage abortion to James Franco, the famous actor. Her argument went something like this. Among early fetuses, there are two different kinds of beings. One has moral status because it is the beginning stage of an actual person. The other doesn't have moral status if it isn't in the early stage of an actual person. What accounts for the distinction? According to Harmon, a fetus has a moral status because it has a future. The aborted fetus doesn't have a moral status because it doesn't have a future. So, she says, if a woman chooses to abort a fetus or suffers a miscarriage, the fetus didn't have moral status. Clearly and understandably puzzled by Harmon's reasoning,

James Franco asked, "Can't you only judge that in hindsight?" He even placed a graphic over top of the video highlighting the circularity of the reasoning. Harmon tried to explain her view more, but did little more than repeat herself. She said the fetus's future "endows moral status on it." What she's argued for, essentially, is a sort of moral time travel. If today a mother chooses to give birth to her baby, then it already had (in the past) moral status when it was an early fetus. But if the mother chooses to abort the baby, the baby never had (in the past) moral status.[24] The puzzled look on James Franco's face was priceless.

Three things have happened here. First, Professor Harmon's otherwise considerable reasoning skills have become confused. Second, she has reduced the human fetus to something that has only extrinsic worth depending on human decisions. Third, she has bestowed upon humans a right and power reserved only for God—to determine whether someone else has value or a future.

Gospel Clarity: Less than God, More than Machine or Beast

After writing 347 pages debunking a purely naturalistic account of humanity, Tallis forthrightly admits that there are no naturalistic answers. "Okay, you might say, you have told us what is wrong with the biological account of human beings but isn't this only the beginning, not the end, of the matter? Now tell us what you will put in its place. *The truth is that I don't know; but I am sure that no one else knows either.*"[25] Atheists like Tallis and Thomas Nagel ask what it means to be human, but find no naturalistic answers. King David, Solomon's father, asked eerily similar questions about what it means to be human as well. Specifically, King David asked God, "What is man that you are mindful of him, and the son of man that you care for him?" (Psalm 8:4). Isn't it fascinating that atheists and theists alike ask the same questions about what it means to be a human with inherent dignity? But Tallis's and Nagel's questions only echo in the silent well of a mindless universe. David and Solomon find a brutally honest yet strangely hopeful answer from the God who made that very universe.

Honesty without Hopelessness: The Desperate Human Heart

Human history, including the graphic history given to us in the Bible, is saturated with evil actions, betrayal, and murder. The Old Testament prophet Jeremiah declares that "the heart is deceitful above all things, and desperately sick; who can understand it?" (Jeremiah 17:9). Jesus echoes those words in Matthew 15:19: "For out of the heart come evil thoughts, murder, adultery, sexual immorality, theft, false witness, slander." Those statements apply to all of us. There are no exemptions. Essentially, Jesus says, "You're evil! Now come, follow me." It's hardly an inviting recruiting slogan. With our cultural desire for unconditional and unceasing affirmation, it's difficult for us to imagine how anyone would have wanted to follow Jesus after he made such disheartening claims about the human heart.

And yet people did follow Jesus by the throngs because his words rang true to his first-century audience. They ought to ring true to us today. With our instant access to information through handheld devices, we can find evidence of human sinfulness at any moment. Better yet, if we honestly search our built-in heart-held devices, we can see what darkness lurks there. To deny human sin is to sin against reason and reality.

One of the many reasons I follow Christ is that his words accurately describe reality. He describes the human heart so spot-on that non-Christians are forced to agree with him. John Gray has typed quite a few words claiming that humanity has been the chief despoiler of itself and the world around it. That's why he won't call humans *Homo Sapiens* but *Homo Rapiens*. And from the religious side of things, the Qur'an acknowledges that human morality is worthy of destructive judgment (Sura 35:45).

Yet while everyone seems to agree with Jesus that humanity has a heart problem, everyone seems to resist the necessary truth that we need redemption from a source outside ourselves. Harvard psychologist and secular humanist Stephen Pinker thinks that as a species, we're getting better—that violence is decreasing and poverty is being addressed. The evidence suggests quite the opposite, actually, which is why John Gray strongly critiques Pinker's optimistic humanism as a "resolute avoidance of inconvenient facts."[26]

Secular humanists like Pinker insouciantly maintain that we can educate ourselves into a better world. Thousands of years of practice ought to pay off soon. Non-Christian religions tell us that if we do enough good works, we can achieve enlightenment, earn God's paradise, or become one with the universe. The Christian faith alone takes the reality and profundity of human sin seriously. Decades before Pinker or Gray, C. E. M. Joad reflected on the nature of human sin and how its oppressiveness ironically gives way to the hope found only in Christ:

> To believe, as I have grown to believe, in the fundamental and in this life ineradicable nature of human sinfulness is intolerable, unless there is some source of guidance and assistance outside ourselves to which we can turn for comfort and assurance. Presently the facts of sin and evil came to present themselves with such overwhelming strength that unless one were able to seek assistance, if not for the overcoming of them, at least for the not succumbing to them, one would give way to despair. The more I knew of it, the more Christianity seemed to offer just that strengthening and assistance. And with that the rationalist-optimist philosophy, by the light of which I had hitherto done my best to live, came to seem intolerably trivial and superficial—a shallow-rooted plant which, growing to maturity amid the lush and leisured optimism of the nineteenth century, was quite unfitted to withstand the bleaker winds that blow through ours. I abandoned it, and in abandoning it found myself a Christian.[27]

If we are inherently sinful—and history proves that we are—we cannot possibly be our own saviors. Like founders of other worldviews, Jesus could have told us that we hold the keys to salvation or deliverance. But Jesus isn't a snake oil salesman who tells you and me what we *want* to hear. He's the consummate realist who tells us what we *need* to hear. But he isn't only a realist, he's also an idealist. He's the realist that John Gray's pessimism might agree with, and he's the idealist that Stephen Pinker's optimism might find attractive.

Salvation Without Compromise: The Cross and Human Dignity

While telling us the inconvenient truth about our sinfulness, Jesus also tells us about the dignity we bear being made in the image of God (Genesis 1:26; Matthew 19:4). Because of that fact, our dignity transcends human opinion and our hope lies beyond any mere human person. Our dignity and hope for redemption lies in God made flesh, the God who took on human form to rescue humanity from itself. The cross is where human depravity and human dignity collide, where the contrarieties of human existence find their resolution. It is where the historical reality of human evil and the historical reality of God's intervention come together. It is at the cross where justice is given and mercy is extended.

It's important that we explore the depth of this paradox for a moment. First, there's the reality of evil and good. For either of these two moral categories to exist objectively, they have to be grounded in a transcendent, personal source. We've already seen how that is so and how leading atheist thinkers agree. But through the gospel, this reality applies in a surprisingly satisfying way. According to the Bible, good and evil don't exist as two opposing yet equal powers. Evil is a perversion of the good, a diminishment of what was intended. C. S. Lewis observed that good is original and evil is merely a perversion, "that good should be the tree and evil the ivy . . . that good should be able to exist on its own while evil requires the good on which it is parasitic."[28]

This means that there is hope for us despite the rapaciousness of our sin. Our good, the Imago Dei in each of us, persists despite our parasitic sin. It means that we can be redeemed and our intended purpose can be restored. It means that we are not stuck being the *Homo Rapiens* John Gray sees us to be.

The cross is the ultimate statement that our moral choices actually matter and that their effects sound into eternity. I can think of no greater respect paid to human beings than that God himself is affected by our moral choices. I remember being asked by a Muslim during an open forum how our actions, even our rejection, could possibly impact the utterly transcendent God. My reply was simply this: If I claimed to love a person, but felt no impact when that person rejected me, how could it be that I truly loved that person? How could it be that the person had any dignity in my eyes if his or her betrayal left me unaffected? The cross is where God demonstrated that sin is so serious and grievous that it has eternal consequences. Jesus' hands, feet, and torso are eternally scarred, showing us that our moral actions have eternal importance. The cross's gravity demonstrates our dignity.

Indeed, the cross goes even further. We return to Peter Singer's rhetorical question: "Why should we believe that the mere fact that a being is a member of the species Homo Sapiens endows its life with some unique, almost infinite value?"[29] If something's value is determined by the price paid for it, then God's answer to Singer is the cross, where an infinite price was paid for each of us.

Resolving the Tension

A signal of the Bible's credibility is the fact that it addresses the tension between humans being made in God's image and humanity being sinful. This tension is not a matter of religious dogma but a fact of life. Tallis's and Pinker's view of humanity's specialness stands in tension with Gray's pessimism. But naturalists have no way to hold the two realities of the human condition in proper tension, and so they must forsake it in favor of one extreme. Jesus' incarnation not only holds the tension but ultimately resolves it.

The intensity of Jesus' suffering on the cross as our substitute shows the depth of our depravity. The fact that God, incarnate in Jesus, subjected himself to that suffering in our place demonstrates our sublime value. The cross blends realism and optimism together. No wonder the hymn writer Isaac Watts wrote that the cross is the place where "sorrow and love flow mingled down." Through that mingling of sorrow and love our depravity is graciously redeemed. Our humanity is restored.

God's incarnation in Christ is itself at once a poetic statement about his majesty and our value. I once heard Bruce Herman of Gordon College talk about art and biblical truth. He pointed out that the Hebrew word we translate as *glory* literally means *weighty* or *heavy*. God uses this word for himself repeatedly throughout the Old Testament. In John 20, we read that Thomas and the disciples were hiding in a locked room following Jesus' crucifixion. In that room, Thomas heard the eyewitness testimony of his comrades that Jesus was raised bodily from the grave. But he remained skeptical. He needed to see Jesus' living body and feel the nail scars and wounded side before he'd believe. It was at that moment that Jesus walked *through* the locked door, even though his resurrected body was physical. After the resurrection his body was both physical and glorified—it was *weighty*. It was weightier than the rest of the physical world around him. C. S. Lewis remarked that Jesus' glorified physical body could pass through a solid door because Jesus was the most real object in the world. He was so weighty, in fact, that a solid wood door was nothing but smoke in comparison.[30]

That's the future hope for each of us in Christ. As he has been raised, the Bible tells us, so we will be. We will have that kind of glorified body as well (1 Corinthians 15:42–49). The gospel tells us that we are not merely physical beings. Nor are we ethereal beings. We are a functional unity of body and soul. Both are important. Both have dignity. It is through God—the transcendent ground of all being—that we have our being (Acts 17:28).

I promised that we'd return to the distinctions in the various forms of the Golden Rule, and so we shall. This Christian message about human dignity is what has made Jesus' formulation of the Golden Rule the United Nation's most popular attraction and the foundation of its charter. All other versions of the Golden Rule are worded in self-protective ways: "Do not do to others what would cause pain if done to you," "Treat not others in ways that you yourself would find hurtful," and so on. These are spiritual versions of pragmatic social contract theory: We refrain from doing bad things so that bad things won't be done to us. We treat others well so that they won't hurt us. But Jesus' wording is subtly, yet profoundly, different. By saying, "Do to others what you would have them do to you," Jesus tells us to treat others well *even if they never treat us well.* Where others advise self-preservation, Jesus encourages self-sacrifice. That shouldn't surprise us coming from the lips of the sacrificial Lamb of God.

Making us dignified, despite the indignities we visit on one another, is an ongoing spiritual process. That's why the Bible describes each of us as God's "workmanship, created in Christ Jesus for good works" (Ephesians 2:10). The two words, *workmanship* and *created*, are not interchangeable. *Workmanship* is translated from the Greek word *poiema*, which means anything brought into existence or compiled by someone. It's where we get the English word *poem* from. You and I—all of us—are God's poem. You were created, but you are still being written, being worked on. The dignity we possess gives meaning to our actions. It gives meaning to our endeavors and aspirations. Judges are not zookeepers and doctors are not mechanics. Even zookeepers and mechanics are more than mere zookeepers or mechanics. We are all poetry. And our finishing stanza will be penned in the coming days' time when all who have embraced Christ will be made new. That dignity is offered to us all. It is a dignity that cannot be muddled or confused by legal opinions or protests.

In the pages that follow, we are going to get into some touchy subjects. As we discuss sexuality, identity, science, and religion, let us do so unto each other as we would want done to us.

CHAPTER 6

Clarity about Sexuality, Gender, and Identity

She walked to the microphone timid yet determined. The question that struggled to free itself from her lips had nothing to do with the evening's topic, yet it couldn't have been more relevant.

That night I joined two colleagues for a university open forum during which we addressed religious pluralism. Stammering a bit through her question, the young lady said, "Sorry if this is off topic, but um, I've searched for answers and I can't seem to find any, so I thought I'd come tonight and ask you guys. Where does Christianity, if it does at all, differ on homosexuality as opposed to other religions, and if so, how?"

The silence of a church on Monday morning momentarily filled the auditorium. Everyone wondered what was going to come out of my mouth next, including me to some extent. I was sure of my position on the matter. But I was unsure of *how* I would convey it. *What will I say that will not compromise biblical sexuality yet show this student that God cares for her beyond measure?*

Of all the topics in this book—and of all the topics I've covered in the numerous debates and open forums in which I've participated—the topics of sexuality and gender identity are by far clouded in the most confusion and emotion. Sexuality is a powerful part of the human experience. It not only pertains to our physical pleasure but also to our emotional well-being. It has a mysterious gravitational tug on our identities. The same is true of gender identity. That's why anger and misunderstanding are such potent factors that keep real conversations from happening. Perhaps that's why the young girl that night walked to the microphone with a quivering lip and trembling hands. She was looking for something so elusive as to be almost ineffable. She was looking for someone to understand her struggle. Understanding doesn't require agreement. It simply requires the kind of empathy that can bridge the gulfs between us. I think of Tom Bracken's poignant words:

> Not understood. We move along asunder;
> Our paths grow wider as the seasons creep
> Along the years; we marvel and we wonder
> Why life is life, and then we fall asleep—
> Not understood.
>
> Not understood. How many breasts are aching
> For lack of sympathy. Ah, day by day,
> How many cheerless, lonely hearts are breaking.
> How many noble spirits pass away—
> Not understood.

O God! that men would see a little clearer,
Or judge less harshly when they cannot see!
O God! that men would draw a little nearer
To one another! They'd be nearer Thee,
And understood.[1]

We must try to understand each other and why our differences exist as the necessary first step toward clarity. I do not here offer a comprehensive treatment of all the issues on these profoundly important topics. In fact, volumes of books have been, and continue to be, written on them. Here my goal is paradoxically modest and ambitious. I hope to point out how the confusion surrounding these issues has kept us at odds and prevented us from truly understanding each other. And I aim to provide clarity about what the gospel says, why it says what it does, and how its message can guide us through our struggles to find God-given identity.

Surveying the Terrain

When it comes to human sexuality and identity, words like *dysphoria*, *confusion*, and *fluid* are ubiquitous. They're even celebrated. What we once thought to be shackles are now lauded as liberating. Our confusion and fluidity have become the hallmarks of our autonomy. Allow me to give an illustration. A few years ago, someone close to me shared that her seventeen-year-old daughter thought she might be a lesbian. Now, both this woman and her daughter are Christians, devotedly so. The seventeen-year-old had significant learning disabilities, yet she was very high functioning. Throughout her school years, she had some friendships, but this new friendship was her first deep one with another female. The newness of the intense connection naturally confused her. She told her mother, "I think I'm a lesbian because I love her." After some time, the mother said, "Of course you love her; I do too. She's a special friend. But that doesn't mean you're a lesbian, honey."

Frustrated and confused, the daughter exploded, "Mom! I love her. I'm gay. I want to be brave too!" And there it was. The young lady had never had a close relationship with another girl before. This happened in the midst of the media frenzy surrounding NFL draft hopeful Michael Sam's announcement that he was gay and Bruce Jenner's announcement that he was transitioning to becoming Caitlin. There was much talk of what heroes they and others like them were. The young girl, dealing with novel emotions, was already awash in the natural confusion that saturates the teen years. The Culture of Confusion powerfully sent her the message that her emotional confusion must mean she's gay and that she would be a hero if she announced it. As it turns out, she would later discover she had misunderstood her feelings.

Though this is just one girl's story, it has much to teach us. The first lesson is that the young girl's honest and caring relationship with her mother allowed her the freedom to share something so tension-inducing. Instead of a screaming match, there was a calm conversation. The mother didn't act out of anger or forbid her daughter from seeing her friend. They walked together through the confusion, allowing it to be just that—a momentary state of adolescent confusion—so that clarity would eventually follow. The Culture of Confusion, on the other hand, seized the moment and told the young girl that same-sex emotional confusion must mean she's gay or bisexual. Now, no one told her that specifically, but the accumulated cultural message influenced her. It's not hard to imagine how younger kids with similar emotional and cognitive development could be just as influenced.

Emotional and sexual confusion no longer just mean confusion. In the contemporary mood, such confusion should lead a person to find themselves in the sexual minority. In fact, the young girl was eager to think that her confusion meant she was gay because being gay is virtuous—it's brave. I recall seeing the crawl on a nearby television announcing that Michael Sam had made the practice squad for the Dallas Cowboys. *How interesting*, I thought. *I can't recall a press conference for someone who only made a team's practice squad.* Sam was becoming a folk hero of sorts because of his bravery in coming out amid a sport known for its testosterone-driven machismo. And so when my friend's daughter thought that being a lesbian would make her a hero, it was quite understandable. Again we see it. Confusion has become a virtue—in this case a heroic one.

Now, one of the reasons that heroism has been ascribed to "coming out" is that people with same-sex attractions have been—and still are—mistreated, sometimes violently. One need look back no further than the evil massacre at the Orlando gay nightclub for evidence that being openly gay still can be dangerous. And so yes, coming out as gay even in today's increasingly accepting and celebratory climate can be an act of bravery.

But the heroism ascribed to being gay or sexually confused makes these identities morally attractive. Instead of being just expressions of one's sexuality, they are seen as expressions of one's virtue. The same tends to be true about gender identity. People who deal with gender dysphoria, the pervasive feeling that one's gender doesn't match their biological sex, are engaged in a genuine, often painful, struggle. Those who eventually choose to identify with a gender *different* from their anatomy are lauded as headline-making heroes. When Bruce Jenner became Caitlin Jenner, ESPN awarded him with the Arthur Ashe Award for Courage. It's interesting that those who resolve their dysphoria by sticking with their bodily sex never make the headlines.

I need to be as clear as I can at this point. I do believe that there are people for whom their same-sex attractions or gender dysphoria are more pervasive and profound than a mere "phase they're going through." It does, in fact, take courage to disclose those feelings to someone else, let alone be public about them. But the point I'm making is that the allure of being labeled a hero can prolong one's confusion and romanticize the struggle instead of showing what it truly is: an arduous, often painful, experience. Those who experience sexual and gender uncertainty still look for ultimate answers, just like the young girl I had the privilege of addressing that night at the university. We owe them more than just making them media darlings and faddish heroes. We owe them compassion and truth.

The problem is that these are such emotion-laden issues that clear thinking, let alone compassionate discussion, is practically impossible, no matter what our perspectives may be. Those on one side become heroes while others become villains in the court of the Culture of Confusion. And that court is fickle, able and eager to switch those labels on a dime.

I have strong convictions on these matters, which probably

is obvious. But I have an even stronger conviction that everyone who engages in, wrestles with, and wants clarity about these subjects is made in God's image. And so it is from that stronger conviction that I wish to proceed.

On Strangely Common Ground

I've never been confused about my sexual preferences or gender. Yet something about another person's struggle for identity resonates with me. Perhaps it's because seventeen years ago, so much about me suddenly changed. For the twenty-seven years prior, I was a proud Muslim, sure that Islam as a religion and Muslims as a community had the answers to life's questions. I shared those answers with non-Muslim friends and invited them to be open-minded about Islam. But when the credibility of classical Christianity confronted me, the gospel I once derided as nonsense looked more credible by the day. And that gospel was telling me something very different about who I am, who God is, what life is about, and where salvation lies. The more solid Christianity's ground became, the more seasick I felt. I simply didn't *want* Christianity to be the fixed point of reference by which my world—especially my identity—was measured. For most of my nine-year search, my identity was simply too much to risk. But as the near decade-long sojourn brought me within an oar's length of the gospel's shoreline, I was beckoned to embrace the gospel no matter the cost. In those last months and weeks, I could hear Jesus, in the voice I imagined him to have, repeating, "Everyone who is of the truth listens to my voice" (John 18:37). Despite the cost, I eventually responded to that voice.

Perhaps that's why the continuing debate over sexual and gender identity stalks my mind and heart. Perhaps that's why I'm sensitive to the turmoil behind the eyes of those who are in the midst of the sexual or gender identity tug-of-war. I think of Rosaria Butterfield, who came to embrace Christianity from a very different background. She was a progressive feminist lesbian. I was a committed Muslim. We both once thought the gospel was silly, even immoral to believe in. Before giving her life to Jesus, Rosaria found contentment with her lesbian partner and meaning from her charity work and LGBT activism. I had found similar fulfillment in my identity as a Muslim. Like me, she began to read the Bible not to believe it, but to debunk it. And also like me, she found its message strangely compelling. We both discovered that the trouble with truth is that it demands something of us. It demands that we yield our desires and desired identities to God's providence and sovereignty. There's hardly a scarier or more difficult thing to do. Two unlikely converts from different backgrounds found themselves to be kindred spirits in the search for truth and identity.

My journey isn't identical to someone who is trying to understand his or her same-sex attractions or gender identity. Yet we may have the common ground of a painful search from which to explore where clarity can be found.

On Strangely Uncommon Ground

The Culture of Confusion's growing obsession with autonomy fuels a movement that encourages us to individually define sexual and gender identity. One might think, then, that the Culture of Confusion is the ally of those with same-sex attractions and gender dysphoria who are still seeking to understand themselves. But that isn't necessarily the case. Some within the Culture of Confusion seek to express their autonomy so as to define away gender altogether, thereby making all sexual expressions permissible. Consider this statement from the International Gay and Lesbian Human Rights Commission:

> For "other sexualities to be possible" it is indispensable and urgent that we stop governing ourselves by the absurd notion that only two possible body types exist, male and female, with only two genders inextricably linked to them, man and woman. We make trans and intersex issues our priority because their presence, activism and theoretical contributions show us the path to a new paradigm that will allow as many bodies, sexualities and identities to exist as those living in this world might wish to have, with each one of them respected, desired, celebrated.[2]

Though this is an extreme position, it shows that at least one advocacy group isn't really focused on bringing resolution to people who deeply feel conflicted about which gender they are. Such conflicted people don't feel genderless or gender fluid. The statement above also shows that choice—not the struggle to understand how we are made—is the real concern, which is why they advocate for as many identities as people "wish to have." Why is it "absurd" to believe there are only two body types, given that, except for an infinitesimal fraction of us, there really are only two body types? Many gender dysphoric people want to resolve their dysphoria in terms of the two binaries of male and female. For them, the binary isn't absurd—it's real.

And why should we encourage "as many sexualities . . . as those living in this world might wish to have"? Odds are that some of those sexualities will be harmful to the people who have them and to others. Ironically, that position makes a mockery of those who feel deeply ingrained but unwanted dysphoria or sexual attractions. They don't necessarily want "as many bodies, sexualities and identities" as possible. They struggle enough to resolve themselves to one body, one identity, and one sexuality. An agenda that pushes for total autonomy breezes past the deep efforts of those with ingrained but unwanted dysphoria or same-sex attractions.

That autonomy above-all-else mentality causes some to rage against the Bible as a repressive tool created by prejudiced, heterosexual, and male-dominated cultures. Some in today's church haven't helped to change that perception much, unfortunately. Over the decades, when sexual ethical issues have become socially prominent, Christians have joined in the *anti* camp. Christians are *anti-same-sex marriage* or *anti-gay*. Same-sex marriage advocates, on the other hand, are seen in the *pro* camp: they are *pro-equality* and *pro-love*. In the rare instances where Christians are in a *pro* posture, they mislabel what it is they're in favor of. Christians have been *pro-traditional marriage* or *pro-biblical marriage*. In other words, Christians tend to be pro-*institution* in their public rhetoric. And there's the problem. The *anti* camp usually loses to the *pro* camp in arenas where hearts and minds are at stake. When there are two *pro* camps, the camp that's in favor of love, people, and rights will usually prevail against the camp that's pro-institution. This is not only true, but also truly sad. If anything, it's the Bible, even with its limitations on sexual expression, that is pro-love and pro-people.

That last statement is undoubtedly very difficult for many to believe. But I will do my best to show why it's true.

Finding the Moral Foundation

Opposition to the Bible's sexual standards is premised on the claim that the Bible is morally capricious. This gives rise to serious questions: *Who are homosexuals or bisexuals hurting? Why can't we just let people love who they want and marry the person they love regardless of their genders?* It mustn't escape us that these are moral questions that assume the existence of an objective, transcendent morality. Jettisoning the Bible from the discussion doesn't get us any closer to such objective answers. In fact, as we've already seen and as I've written elsewhere, if we evict all transcendent sources of moral authority, there are no objective moral answers. Relying on our own ever-shifting opinions as the foundation of sexual ethics courts chaos and uncertainty. What is acceptable today may be repugnant tomorrow. And so to even begin asking whether there should be any boundaries to sexuality and identity is to implicitly rely on the very God we might rebel against or claim doesn't exist.

The young girl's question at the university open forum that night was a moral one for which she sought objectively true answers. So we explored the issue together based on that common ground. To do this as a Christian means first taking a hard look at how our actions and reactions on these issues have been so *immoral*. Yes, there has been an erosion of religious freedom when it comes to this issue. And yes, it can be very difficult to speak and act compassionately when stigmatized as a hater or bigot, especially when one tries their best to follow the Christian ethic of unconditional love, but not unconditional affirmation. To deal with the rising resentment, we have to embrace the Christian moral virtue of uncompromising understanding. It's unfortunately something violated every day through the vice of hypocrisy. Homosexuality, bisexuality, and transgenderism have become the issues of the day. But some Christians' reactions have turned them into the only or worst sins of the day. For some it's as if these are the only aspects of the human condition for which Christ did not die.

Many may bristle when Christians equate homosexuality with sins committed by heterosexuals. It's unfair, they might say, to view a loving, monogamous gay relationship to be as sinful as an extramarital affair by a heterosexual spouse. There are two responses to this. First, according to the Bible, same-sex behavior is sinful. There is simply no sugarcoating that, no matter how many hermeneutical gymnastics some may employ.[3] We'll address why the Bible calls it sinful—and what that really means—shortly. But second, acknowledging same-sex sex as sinful expresses nothing more, but nothing less, than this: all of us are fractured *in every way*, including *but not limited to* our sexuality. Every person—whether same-sex attracted or not, whether conflicted about his or her gender or completely sure of it—has veered from our originally intended purpose. We're broken in different ways, but we are broken together. Together we need restoration.

When Christians think of others as more broken than them, they flirt with an unbalanced view of biblical sexuality and the sinfulness of humanity. So many Christians seem to forget their own brokenness in self-righteously judging those with same-sex attractions. I find this so very odd because the gospel is good news for sinners, not the righteous. I recognized my need for a savior because I realized that I stood as morally inadequate before God as any other human being. How then can I say that anyone else, regardless of whether I disagree with them, is somehow less human, or less redeemable, than I am? Yes, we can legitimately judge behaviors and ideas as moral or immoral, true or false. But we dare not judge other people's value to God.

The imbalance runs in both directions. LGBT advocates think the Christian God, and thus conservative Christians, are obsessed with sexual prohibitions. Christians perpetuate this by shouting biblical passages prohibiting certain sexual expressions. It may surprise both camps to know that there are only a relative handful of passages about sexual morality and same-sex behavior. That doesn't limit the gravamen of those passages but, as my friend and colleague Sam Allberry says, "At the very least this does show us that the Bible is not fixated on homosexuality. It is not what the Bible is 'about.'"[4]

This imbalance has resulted in the modern heterosexual-homosexual identity paradigm, which makes us focus on people who have certain sexual identities as more or less sinful or broken than others. This not only hinders a meaningful conversation about sexual and gender ethics, it also creates an "us versus them" battleground whereby we see "us" as the moral paragons and "them" as pariahs. In an article entitled "Against Heterosexuality," Michael Hannon makes some interesting points, namely that the idea of sexual orientation is unhelpful in understanding how to clearly work toward sexual morality. He points out that same-sex attracted progressives like Michel Foucault and others think that sexual orientation is not an objective reality of human existence, but only a social construct. Such progressives want to see sexual orientation deconstructed so that there are no norms to conform to—heterosexual, homosexual, or otherwise—thereby allowing us unfettered sexual autonomy. While Hannon agrees that sexual orientation is a social construct, he says that getting rid of it shouldn't result in a world without sexual norms, but in a world that primarily focuses us on God-given identity. Otherwise, we misjudge others as perpetually sinful when it comes to sex and ourselves as perpetually virtuous. "The most pernicious aspect of the orientation-identity systems is that it tends to exempt heterosexuals from moral evaluation," Hannon writes. "If homosexuality binds us to sin, heterosexuality blinds us to sin."[5]

Hannon's point is that orientation labels prevent us from actually looking inward to see our own sin. That's ironic, of course, because labels are meant to clear things up. But in this context, they blind us from seeing our true originally intended identities and how far we've all veered from that original intention. I've often wondered if those who spew vitriol at "the other" take the time to clear their web-browser history before doing so. Clearing a browser history isn't the same as clearing a conscience. The windows to all of our souls need cleaning from a source outside of ourselves.

This is not to say, of course, that we can't look at the objective standard that God gives to us for sexuality, or that we can't judge actions as right or wrong, beneficial or harmful. In fact, we have to. But when we bifurcate sexuality into the supposedly unbroken (heterosexual) and the broken (everyone else), we make ourselves the arbiters of right, wrong, beneficial, and harmful. Although I don't agree with everything she writes,

Jenell Williams Paris is right in saying that "even humble Christians who make every effort to be kind and gracious toward homosexuals are not really reaching out; they're reaching down from a place of moral elevation."[6] In recent years, with the massive cultural shift away from conservative views on sexuality, same-sex affirming people have set up their own moral high horses, feeling themselves to be free of bigotry and hatred, reaching down to Bible thumping Neanderthals to enlighten them about twenty-first century ethics. The fact is that we are all bent rulers trying to judge others as crooked. We need the objective standard, the unbent guideline, by which we evaluate others' behavior, especially our own. Christopher Yuan is a devoted Christian who experiences same-sex attractions but submits them in celibacy before Christ. He passionately urges us to strive not for heterosexuality, but "holy sexuality." To understand holy sexuality is to understand that "desire warrants discipline and care, not fulfillment and affirmation."[7] This is a journey each of us is on. Ideally, we should be on it together. "The journey toward sexual holiness is for all people," Paris says. "No one has a head start, especially by virtue of feelings they didn't even choose."[8] I'm convinced that it is the biblical worldview, in distinction to others, that provides the needed objective standard.

Only So Many Paths to Choose From

That night of the open forum, the young lady asked her question in the context of my colleague's presentation on major world religions. She had looked everywhere, she said, but hadn't found the answer she needed. I admired her search, her willingness to look for answers wherever they might be. The pathos in her voice and behind her eyes revealed that she wasn't just looking for yet another opinion. She wanted an answer that would validate who she was as a human being. I wonder if she realized just how astute and profound her question was. Her question assumed that every worldview—not just Christianity—has to address sexuality in coherent, yet humanity dignifying ways. What I suggested was that there are only so many worldviews to choose from. And none of them provide her with answers that unconditionally validate her humanity. That is, except for one.

Consider naturalistic atheism first. Logically speaking, it can't offer that young lady any answers that validate her same-sex attractions. It continues to surprise me that naturalists seem to be so supportive of LGBT causes despite the fact that same-sex sexuality seems so "unevolutionary." Richard Dawkins famously wrote that "human beings are simply machines for propagating DNA, and the propagation of DNA is a self-sustaining process. It is every living object's sole reason for living."[9] As a Christian, I categorically disagree with him. If Dawkins is correct that human beings have no purpose higher than breeding, same-sex sex violates (or at least doesn't serve) that biological purpose. If our sole purpose is to transmit DNA into the next generation as naturalism implies, then same-sex sex, which has no chance of doing that, is naturalism's cardinal sin.

Can the pantheistic religions offer the young lady something that validates her sexuality? In the West, we tend to think that pantheistic religions like Hinduism and Buddhism are tolerant and open to a variety of sexual expressions. After all, these are the religious traditions that gave us the *Kama Sutra*, tantric sex, and the like. But approximately ten years ago, the Indian Prince Manvendra Singh Gohil publicly declared his homosexuality, only to be met with public hostility. His wealthy family disowned him, his own mother declaring in a paid advertisement that "henceforth no one must refer to my name as mother of Manvendra. If any individual or organization does so, it will invite contempt proceedings."[10] Eastern pantheism's tolerance has some very serious cultural limitations.

Could the young lady have looked to pantheism's Western versions, specifically the New Age or the spirituality of Deepak Chopra and others like him? When scrutinized, their foundations are incredibly flimsy. They teach that morality is relative and suffering is an illusion, so if someone with same-sex attractions is looking for objective validation, they won't find it there. All one can find is strained relativistic talk about self-actualization and personal growth.

And then, of course, there is the path Islam offers. While Islam is a monotheistic religion that shares some ethical ideas with the Judeo-Christian view, Islam is openly and judicially antagonistic to homosexuality. In fact, in many Islamic countries, the young lady couldn't even have asked her question in public without risking grave reprisal. Indeed, homosexual behavior carries with it the death penalty in some Islamic countries.

Does the Gospel Offer a Better Path?

Having considered and exhausted those religious (and nonreligious) paths that night, we came to the Christian worldview. Some protest that the Bible's narrow-minded statements on same-sex behavior similarly disqualify it from offering true validation of the breadth of human sexuality. The critic of Christianity's sexual ethics will trot out well-known Bible passages about homosexuality. "You shall not lie with a male as with a woman; it is an abomination" (Leviticus 18:22; 20:13). And so the critic asks, *How can the Bible validate the sexuality of someone whose sexual orientation the Bible calls abominable?* From Leviticus to Romans to 1 Corinthians, these passages are "Exhibit A" in the critic's prosecution of Christianity's allegedly arbitrary sexual repressions.

Some have tried to rationalize away or reinterpret the Bible's clear statements on same-sex behavior to the extent that the clear statements become meaningless. They have argued that the Bible prohibits nonconsensual same-sex behavior, not loving, monogamous homosexuality.[11] Others discount the Bible as a source of sexual moral authority and instead embrace human autonomy. Better to rely on our own sense of selfhood and define the boundaries, they would argue. Sexuality, after all, is intensely private, resulting from each person's feelings. No arbitrary rules should bind our self-understanding.

But is it really true that the Bible's statements on sexuality are arbitrary and freedom restricting? Many who reject biblically defined sexuality seem to understand *what* the Bible says about same-sex desires and behavior, but they have flawed assumptions about *why* the Bible says what it does. In a culture that increasingly thinks of sex as recreational, the fact that the Bible puts boundaries on sex seems arbitrary. Western culture is replete with sentiments like *casual sex* and *hooking up*. We seem so cavalier in saying that an encounter was "just sex." I recall at an open forum on sexuality a panelist, speaking on behalf of a campus LGBT group, responded to the question, "What does sex mean to you?" with the answer, "It depends on who I am having it with."

But we cannot get away from our intuitive perception that there's something about sex that goes beyond the merely physical. There's a reason why the law recognizes the difference between physical assault and *sexual* assault. We have one reaction when we are told someone was beaten. We have quite another reaction when we are told that someone was raped. Assault victims may experience emotional trauma. But rape victims take multiple showers after being violated, only to have their sullied feeling remain. Assault victims are beaten. Rape victims are *violated*. There is something sacredly fragile about sexuality. And that which is fragile and sacred needs boundaries to protect it.

Of course, there are equivocal uses of the word *sacred*. Different religions consider different days or objects sacred. And in that sense, sacredness can be subjective. But sacredness has an objective sense as well. That which is objectively or inherently sacred cannot be merely sacred *to me* or *to you*. Otherwise, it isn't inherently sacred. It's only incidentally sacred. Human sexuality can only be objectively sacred if its substance and expression do not depend on the vagaries of human opinion and perceived autonomy. When sacredness loses its objective sense, that which we once held to be sacred becomes common and profane. It loses that which makes it special and beautiful. We sacrifice sacredness on the altar of sexual autonomy.

Within us is a yearning to see sexuality as more than common sport. With alcohol, drugs, or gambling, the addictions are fed with just more alcohol, drugs, or gambling. People addicted to pornography, however, feed their addiction not with just more pornography, but with different, increasingly exotic pornography.[12] What once tantalized becomes common. So an addict searches for something new. But after a time, the newly found allurement becomes common as well. The search for the next enticement begins, and so the cycle perpetuates. This is what can happen when we seek out multiple sexual partners and casual sex. Even in the skewed perception of addiction or casualized sex, our inner longing for ultimate satisfaction beckons us. I offered to the young lady that evening that God wants to protect the sacredness of her sexuality from becoming common. The boundaries provided in God's Word can give her sexuality sublimity once again.

Protecting, Not Just Prohibiting

This is key to understanding why God says what he does about sexuality, marriage, and identity. Indeed, this is really my main focus: getting clarity about *why* the Bible says what it does so that we can get clarity on *who* the Bible says we are. God isn't arbitrarily prohibiting certain conduct; he is *protecting* something sacred. Carefully consider Paul's words in Romans 1:24–27 in which he writes that sex outside the bounds of opposite-sex marriage "dishonors" the body and results from "dishonorable passions." At first reading, it seems hard to see the protection of the sacred in these passages. They sound like harsh judgments. But to whom are the sexual acts dishonoring? They dishonor not only God but also those who engage in them. The resolution comes in 1 Corinthians 6:9–11 where Paul writes to fellow believers who once engaged in the prohibited actions. He tells them that having found their true identity in Christ, they have been *washed, sanctified,* and *justified.* Their honor has been restored. The boundaries God has placed on sexuality are there to protect its sacredness and, in turn, our sacredness.

The Sacredness of Sexuality

How does limiting sexuality to opposite-sex marriage do that exactly? To unravel this mystery, we must recall what it means to be made in God's image. "So God created man in his own image, in the image of God he created him; *male* and *female* he created *them*" (Genesis 1:27, emphasis added). Those words are both marvelous and unique. Orthodox Islam would never espouse such an idea. Indeed, Islam considers it blasphemous to say that in some way we bear God's image. We would never hear such a statement from a pantheist, who doesn't view us as bearing God's image but as being one with the impersonal divine force. And we certainly wouldn't hear a naturalist claim that each of us bears the image of a God who doesn't exist.

Human sacredness leads us to see why human sexuality is sacred and worth protecting. When we fawn over a baby, we're not coldly observing a mere organism. We're beholding the cheek-dominated visage of one who bears divine fingerprints. Sex between a man and a woman is the only means by which such a precious being comes into this world.[13] And because a human being is the sacred product of sex, the sexual process by which that person is made is also sacred.

There is still further depth to the sublimity of biblical sexuality. Not only is sex sacred because it produces sacred beings but also because it affords us the joyous privilege of reflecting on something beautiful about God himself. God, as the ground of all being, is also the grounding of all knowledge. It's fascinating that the Bible describes the first human sexual encounter with language that reflects this: "Now the man *knew* his wife Eve, and she conceived and bore Cain, saying, 'I have produced a man with the help of the LORD'" (Genesis 4:1–2, NRSV, emphasis added). Human sexuality is about *knowing* another person. Animal sex is based on mere procreative instinct. But human sex is about knowledge. Indeed, the capacity for knowledge is part of what it means to bear God's true image. And the creative aspect, to produce another life with God's help, shows the sacred splendor of what sexuality was meant to be.

There's another, perhaps more primordial, reflection of the divine with which we are privileged. The bonds of marriage between one man and one woman frame the beautiful portrait of unity in diversity. From our chromosomal and hormonal differences to our diverse proclivities and temperaments, men and women are gloriously different. Our disparities have the power to both drive us mad and spark our laughter. The differences between the sexes are the stuff of sitcoms, romance novels, Shakespearean plays, and our everyday lives.

Why do we cherish this kind of unity in diversity? A clue lies in understanding our origins. As contingent beings, our existence is explained by a cause beyond ourselves. And the best explanation of why we—the effect—crave relationships and delight in the unified diversity of relationships is that God—our Cause—exists as an eternally unified diversity in the community of the Trinity. In Christianity, God exists as one being, but with three divine and distinct personhoods or centers of consciousness. The Father is God, but the Son is also

God, and so is the Holy Spirit. They all share the same divine nature—they are all the same and single *what*. Yet the Father, Son, and Holy Spirit are distinct personhoods or centers of consciousness. They are three distinct *whos*. There is unity in diversity in the very source of all that exists. This explains why we—as the creations of God—value unity in diversity so much. In fact, we champion diversity in our cultures when we demand it in the workplace, on television shows, and in our schools. Nothing explains this human longing better than the divine Trinity.

Sexuality within a one-man-and-one-woman marriage expresses and reflects that unity in diversity. Despite their diversity, men and women miraculously come together to create a bond of fidelity to one another. A smile parts our lips when we see an elderly couple walking arm in arm in a park or sitting on a bench with hands intertwined. This is more than mere sentimentality at two old people being "cute." It inspires us because their wrinkles map the long, unified journey of two fundamentally diverse people. My wife's grandparents celebrated seventy years of marriage before her grandmother recently passed away. In those seven decades, they forsook romances with all others to seal their diverse unity.

The Bible says that "a man shall leave his father and his mother and hold fast to his wife, and they shall become one flesh" (Genesis 2:24). Fascinatingly, the Hebrew word *echad* translated as *one* in this oft-quoted verse does not actually mean the number "1." It literally means *unity*. And so we can rightly understand this verse describing biblical marriage to mean "and they shall become *unified* flesh." Jesus repeats this passage when describing marriage's sacredness. "Have you not read," he says, "that he who created them from the beginning made them male and female, and said, 'Therefore a man shall leave his father and his mother and hold fast to his wife, and the two shall become one flesh'? So they are no longer two but one flesh. What therefore God has joined together, let not man separate" (Matthew 19:4–6). Jesus specifically says that God made humanity diverse—*male and female*—and *therefore* they will become one flesh. Jesus tells us that diversity is the foundation of unity, and unity is the foundation of marriage.

We are given the privilege through opposite-sex marriage to reflect the unity in diversity of God, who is the foundation of reality. From this we can begin to see that God-ordained sexuality and marriage secure the importance and dignity of established binary genders. God refers to himself in masculine pronouns and labels: He is God the Father, God the Son, King of Kings, and so on. But he also self-refers in feminine aspects: "O Jerusalem, Jerusalem," Jesus says. "How often would I have gathered your children together as a hen gathers her brood under her wings" (Matthew 23:37, Luke 13:34). God has given us birth (Deuteronomy 32:18), and God comforts us as a mother comforts her children (Isaiah 66:13). The miraculous unification of diversity that Jesus describes marriage to be doesn't work unless there are two diverse partners. The two genders aren't interchangeable. If you're a man, you are vital to the unification of sexuality and marriage *because* you're male and not female. If you're a woman, you are indispensable *because* you are female and not male.

There's yet more depth to the sacredness of biblical sexuality. Unity in diversity not only undergirds all of creation but also consummates in God's redemptive plan for humanity. The

Bible tells us that in the culmination of history, a great wedding takes place. The body of believers is repeatedly referred to as the "bride of Christ." And God himself, majestic and mighty, yet gentle as a lamb, will marry that bride. The relationship that began between God and humanity in the garden of Eden—a relationship we marred and distorted—will finally be restored. And a wedding is the picture of that restoration that God has given to us (Revelations 19:7–9).

That wedding is another beautiful portrait of unity in diversity as the expression of human value and meaning. God—the eternal, perfect, pure, all-knowing, and all-powerful being—spiritually marries humanity—the temporal, imperfect, tainted, limited creatures that we are. It is as diverse a pairing as could be, and yet through the unity of the diverse, we are transformed and purified. God has chosen marriage between a man and a woman to foreshadow the ultimate reconciliation of humanity to himself. God made us for covenant relationship with him because he himself is a triune being in relationship. Unity in diversity forms the bookends of eternity. It exists in the uncaused Creator of all things and is the state in which we will exist forever. Biblical sexuality and marriage reflect that beauty.

Whether one has opposite-sex or same-sex attractions, whether one is confident in his or her gender or feels confused about it, God anchors human dignity and sacredness in the unchanging eternal. That's why the Bible says what it says about all sexual expressions outside of monogamous, opposite-sex marriage. God is protecting something sacred and beautiful. We are given the honor of reflecting an aspect of the divine splendor. That's why Paul says that same-sex behavior "dishonors" us—it takes us away from what God bestows (see Romans 1:26). Our sanctity is restored to us when we strive to reflect the divine once again (1 Corinthians 6:11). God wants that beauty and sacredness for each of us—whether we are dealing with infidelity, emotional betrayals, addictions, or same-sex attractions.

Yes, *all of us*. Regardless of the attitudes we may have seen from Christians (whether winsome or repugnant), the Bible shows us that God is not *anti* something for no reason. Sam Allberry is so right: "What the Bible says about homosexuality does not represent everything God wants to say to homosexual people."[14] God's statements about sexuality are not only strong protections of our sacredness but also instructions by which we prepare ourselves for what he has in store for each of us. And as I shared that truth with the young woman at the public forum that night, clarity about what God says about sexuality, why he says it, and what it offers us dawned. Connecting with the need Tom Bracken identified in his poem, she seemed to know she was "understood." The tears began to flow, and she afforded me the honor of praying with her.

Sanctity in Singleness

These realizations about why the Bible says what it says and what it seeks to protect won't necessarily make our desires or attractions instantly melt away. For the majority of people, they linger. In fact, those who don't have same-sex attractions continue to struggle with infidelity, sex addiction, or pornography even after coming to understand the sacredness of sexuality. What then for those whose same-sex attractions persist? Are they doomed to a life of loneliness, never to have romance?

This is not something to be flippant about. Christopher Yuan and Sam Allberry have addressed it in some detail and with a compassion born of their own singleness. These two men, in addition to another friend and colleague, David Bennett, have submitted their desires and attractions to Christ. Though their longings have not changed, they bear their crosses every single day, making Jesus the center of their lives. That kind of sacrifice is worth marinating in for just a moment. Think of it: one of the most powerful longings in the human heart is for romantic attachment. Many of us have a hard time resisting fast food or giving up bad habits for our own good or to honor God. But these men, and thousands of people like them, submit their deepest desires to Christ not just on a daily basis, but on a moment-by-moment basis. How many of us, whether Christian or not, can say that we've had such constancy of devotion to anything or anyone? Those people are heroes to me.

Even with their daily sacrifices, they don't see themselves as condemned to an unfair life of loneliness. In fact, none of us, whether opposite-sex or same-sex attracted, is guaranteed a life devoid of loneliness. Same-sex attracted people may yearn for a mate, yet they may not get into just any relationship to punctuate the loneliness, especially if the relationship may dishonor God. Earthly human marriage isn't our savior. God himself is our Savior, not our relationships with each other. Human marriage and sexuality are meant to reflect the coming unity of diversity in the celestial marriage offered to each of us. Engaging in same-sex sex downplays that unity in diversity and serves as a sort of earthly distraction from the eternal unity of diversity to come.

The romantic-comedy era has caused Christians and non-Christians alike to view singleness as immature, neurotic, or inhumane. Contemporary culture also tells us that we *are* our desires—whatever they may be—and that if we don't fulfill them, we won't be fully ourselves. As Christopher Yuan points out, we wrongly think single people are socially broken, which is why we're always trying to "fix them up" with someone. It's fascinating that the two most influential people in history, Jesus and the apostle Paul, were single. Neither of them was socially or emotionally broken. In describing heaven, Jesus points out that we will neither be married nor given in marriage. We are to be in relationship with God. The Bible tells us that God's judgment of the world will be followed by a wedding of Christ to his bride, which is the church (Mark 2:19–20; 2 Corinthians 11:2; Revelation 19:9, 21:2–3). We are not going to be married to each other in heaven because marriage—which is a reflection of our intended relationship with the Creator—will no longer be needed. We won't need the mirror when we are looking squarely into the divine visage.

Romantic and sexual desires don't define us. Nor does sexual attraction. It is God who defines us. We only find that identity through repentance. King David found his identity when he repented of his adultery. A woman may find her identity when she repents of viewing the "perfect romance" as life's ultimate goal. A gay man or woman may find his or her identity when they repent for making their sexual orientation their defining characteristic. I found my identity when I repented of so many broken thoughts, including making religious piety my identity.

Clarity about Gender and Identity

"No one is satisfied with anyone else's perspective on the topic of gender identity," writes Mark A. Yarhouse in his book *Understanding Gender Dysphoria*.[15] He's right, of course. This topic has erupted into a global conversation with such rapidity that it's almost impossible to get a handle on it. Aside from the flood of gender pronouns, there are terms like *transgender, transsexual, gender dysphoria, intersex, cisgender,* and others too numerous to list here.[16] Clarity on this tough subject comes when we maintain our focus to see that we must address two different but related phenomena. Transgenderism, like sexuality, is simultaneously a genuine struggle some people go through and a bobble exploited by those who want unfettered autonomy. Thus, the motivations for discussing and even advocating for acceptance of transgenderism are different. Both need a clear response. How to offer that clarity with uncompromising compassion is the real trick.

On the one hand, there are those who are struggling through a legitimate, diagnosable condition of gender dysphoria. For such people, the dysphoria is an unwanted and psychological stressor. They want nothing more than to get clarity about who they are. Gender dysphoria is a subset of the broader term *transgender*. When we think of transgender people, we think of someone who is biologically one sex but thinks of himself as the other sex. But transgender people may include those who like to dress in clothing of the opposite sex and have no desire to change their physical bodies. And, according to the new lexicon, someone may be transgender because they identify as *gender fluid*, which means that they believe their gender is not fixed as either male or female. They can change between genders (or experience both) depending on the circumstances.

Gender dysphoria used to be included in the American Psychiatric Association's Diagnostic and Statistical Manual (DSM) under the term "Gender Identity Disorder." Today, the DSM's fifth edition removes the word "disorder" and describes the same condition under the label Gender Dysphoria. A simple definition of gender dysphoria is: "The experience of distress associated with the incongruence wherein one's psychological and emotional gender identity does not match one's biological sex."[17] For the most part, those with gender dysphoria don't think of themselves as fluidly exercising their autonomy to identify with the gender (or nongender or pangender) of their choice. Try as they might, they have been unable to shake the feeling that their minds are one sex but their bodies are another. Of course there is a spectrum about how strongly a particular person feels. But the fact is that these precious people typically are not looking for a genderless or gender-fluid society. They are dealing with something incredibly personal and painful.

Transgenderism's explosive prevalence in the media gives one the impression that gender dysphoria is a relatively common phenomenon. But from the most recent estimates, only between 0.005 and 0.014 percent of adult males and between 0.002 and 0.003 percent of adult females have gender dysphoria. Other studies suggest that the prevalence of gender dysphoria is between 1 in 10,000 to 1 in 13,000 males and 1 in 20,000 to 1 in 34,000 females.[18] In other words, genuine gender dysphoria is quite rare. And so at least part of what's causing the media attention isn't the real plight of a significant portion of the population. What's driving a lot of it is the Culture of Confusion's desire for autonomy. The few who truly deal with gender dysphoria have become the mascots for autonomy-obsessed people who don't actually have dysphoria. I realize the following is an extreme statement, but when Miley Cyrus called herself *pansexual* or even "a genderless soul," she wasn't experiencing any sense of dysphoria. She was expressing her desire to autonomously self-identify. There is a vast difference between that kind of agenda and an agenda that seeks the well-being of those with genuine gender dysphoria. A crucial step toward clarity on this issue is understanding that important distinction.

They Don't Choose Dysphoria

Again, clarity comes and the fissures are healed when we are understood. And so it's critical to be clear on this: gender dysphoria is a real condition. When it pervades beyond childhood, it's not a fist-clenched, willful rebellion against the way God made that person. My sensitivity for the struggles of those experiencing gender dysphoria was heightened when I read something from Mark Yarhouse. In a counseling session with a young woman who has gender dysphoria, Yarhouse said to her, "I don't think you chose to experience your gender incongruence." That stunned her. She had seen multiple pastors, all of whom said or implied that she chose to be dysphoric and was in sinful rebellion. Having someone finally realize that she didn't choose to feel that way was nothing short of revolutionary.[19] Andrew Walker, a conservative Christian, rightly observes that "individuals who experience gender dysphoria are not sinning when such experiences occur. To feel that your body is one sex and your self is a different gender is not sinful. The Bible nowhere categorizes unwanted psychological distress as sinful in itself."[20]

These statements ought to shock some of us out of our misunderstandings and insensitivities, especially since they have led to mistreatment. When Christians mistake genuine dysphoria for willful rebellion, the mistreatment comes in the form of either unwarranted judgment or exclusion from church—the one place where people should be able to find their true identity in Christ. When the autonomy-obsessed among us view gender as a matter of choice, the mistreatment takes the form of minimizing (or even trivializing) the real anguish those with dysphoria go through.

There are real, grimly permanent consequences to our willing confusion of this issue. People with a genuine dysphoria experience the gamut of emotional upheavals, from depression to anger to suicidal thoughts. When we belittle them, calling them names for having their unwanted dysphoria, we exacerbate those emotions. But the same holds true for dealing with the dysphoria by encouraging sex reassignment surgery. One would think that once a person's body is surgically and hormonally changed to match their mental gender feelings, the dysphoria would dissolve and the person would be happier. But that simply isn't the case. Several peer-reviewed studies have revealed that transgender people who undergo sex reassignment surgery experience far higher death rates than the rest of the populace. In fact, transsexuals experience shockingly higher rates of suicide *after* having sex reassignment surgery.[21] The consequences of getting this issue wrong are dire indeed.

Why ignore these grim facts and persist in changing the body rather than addressing the mind when there is incongruence between the two? Because in the post-truth Culture of Confusion, we elevate preferences over facts and truth. We will adapt reality according to our preferences, not the other way around. In fact, we do this quite literally to death. If conservatives or Christians mistreat people with gender dysphoria to prop up their sense of self-righteousness, progressives mistreat them to advance their agenda of autonomy. Amid the confusion, those with real identity struggles are forgotten. Christ alone knows who we are through and through. And because of that each one of us in our fractured states needs to come to him. That doesn't guarantee that everything will be fine at the instant of belief. But if Jesus is the one who makes all things new—and his resurrection from the dead proved that he is— then we will find congruence and wholeness either in this life or in the next. We will be understood. That's not a matter of mere preference. It is a matter of fact.

I witnessed the power of this message in early 2017 during a public dialogue at McGill University. Sam Allberry was paired with Michelle Li, the leader of the LGBTQ group on campus. As the venue was filling to capacity, I sat in the back observing the attendees' faces and language. To say that the tension was palpable would be an understatement.

The evening began with Ms. Li discussing the first time she felt same-sex attractions, how her family dealt with it, and so on. Then it was Sam's turn. When he was asked about the first time he realized he felt same-sex attractions, there was an audible gasp in the room. No one expected it. They thought that they were going to hear a Bible thumper talk about fire, brimstone, and sodomites. But they didn't. They heard an understanding and compassionate, yet biblically uncompromised voice. During the question-and-answer period, a transgender girl came to the microphone, her hostility still not abated. She angrily asked Sam why she should want to come to a church whose very existence was based on a morally corrupt book that fueled the hate of homophobic, transphobic misogynists. It was a scathing indictment.

Sam's response was unforgettable: "I'm heartbroken that you feel that way, all the more because it's likely that Christians are the ones who made you feel that way." He went on to explain what it means to be broken as a human being, that all of us are broken together in more ways than just our sexuality or genders. After some exchange between them, the student said something remarkable: "I think you would be an amazing father and an amazing husband to someone." Sam in no way compromised God's original design of humanity with its binary genders. Nor did he compromise biblical sexuality. And yet the Holy Spirit worked in the heart and mind not only of that precious girl but also in the hearts and minds of quite a few other people who were expecting a fight but instead found compassion and respect.

This is what it means to be uncompromising yet inviting. People are struggling, they're hurt, and they're angry. The only antidote to it all is a biblically faithful compassion. The church needs to open its doors and Christians need to open their hearts so that those struggling to find resolution to their dysphoria—and those who are struggling to find clarity amidst other confusions—can find community and, ultimately, their true identity in Christ. In Christ, they can be understood.

The Hard Road of Finding Clarity and Congruence

This may all sound very well-meaning, but can true identity be achieved for any of us, let alone those struggling with gender dysphoria? Again, it starts with the understanding that we are all valuably made in God's image. The next step is to understand the interconnectedness of our minds and our bodies. Christianity is unfairly caricatured as an otherworldly religion, a belief system that cares more about the soul than the body. It will surprise many people to realize that this is actually a heresy of the Christian faith known as Gnosticism. It was the Gnostics who considered the body to be a corrupt or evil thing and that the soul (or the mind) is the pure self. Orthodox Christianity, on the other hand, will have none of that. Jesus didn't rise spiritually from the dead. He rose bodily. His body is perfectly glorified. And when those who are in Christ are raised, their souls will join their glorified physical bodies for eternity in restoration. God's original intent is for harmony between one's soul and one's body. This is why Christians, of all people, should be compassionately concerned with helping people find mind-body congruence.

But, someone might say, non-Christians are just as concerned, which is why they advocate for hormone injections or sex reassignment surgery to change someone's body to conform to their mental gender identity. This really is the Gnostic approach all over again. The Gnostics believed that the mind should dominate the body, not work in harmony with it. Today, someone's mental experience of being one gender is considered the valid experience. If the body doesn't agree, we change the body to fit the mind. It is an unfortunately myopic view, especially since changing the body has negative consequences. For the Christian, the mind and the body are both important and were meant to work harmoniously.

This biblical perspective defends our integrity as whole human beings in contradistinction to the secular effort to reduce us to our chemistry and jettison any idea that we have an immaterial mind or soul. If we are mere machines, then we can see why some think that the body should be conformed to the psychological gender experience. The mind and the body are actually the same thing, after all, so the body has no precedence over the mind. In fact, one might argue, there is no "mind" to change.

No one really knows what causes gender dysphoria. One theory is called the Brain-Sex Theory and has many interpretations. This theory basically posits that male and female brains are structurally and chemically different. During fetal development, a person's female brain structure or chemistry remains the same while their body develops into a male (and vice versa at times). Thus, a person is biologically dysphoric. Now, one day we may find that there is some merit to this theory. Regardless, an important point remains: *we are not our brains.* Any attempt to reduce the struggle over gender identity to brain structure and biochemistry is an illegitimate attempt to reduce us to mere meat computers once again.

That's why the invitation of Christ has come in this order:

recognition, repentance, redemption, regeneration. When we recognize our need for the Savior (because of our sins in general, not because of our dysphoria), repentance happens and then we are redeemed. But that redemption works itself out in our lives over time. It is the Holy Spirit who lives and works in us to conform us to Jesus' likeness. It is not an overnight process, which means the church needs to do a better job of helping that process along. The church needs to foster community. It can be quite painful to do so, especially when there are such sensitive issues at play. But it is always worth it.

With that regeneration of our spirit comes the change of identity. I don't mean that we lose one true identity and gain another true identity. No, what I mean is that we shed our artificial, fractured identities, those that we and the world have constructed for ourselves, so that we can gain a restored identity in Christ.

Liberty through Our Bonds

I have never struggled with same-sex attractions, nor have I felt incongruence between the gender I feel that I am and my bodily sex characteristics. And yet I feel a surprising kinship with those who do. Before I became a Christian, my identity was steeped in the religion of Islam. When I encountered the truth of the gospel, that Jesus is who the Bible says he is, my mind cascaded into a spiritual identity dysphoria. That's why the journey to Christ took nine years for me. The truth wasn't hard to find. It was hard to embrace.

I empathize, therefore, with what it means to take one's profoundly felt identity and desires and submit them to Christ—to crucify them every day and then carry that cross. Matt Moore powerfully describes the ongoing process and why it is worth the effort. His article "I Begged God to Make Me Straight and He Never Answered" is profoundly worded so I quote it at length:

> I wanted God to take away my same-sex desires for my own benefit—so that I could fit in, be normal, be one of the guys, and even so that I could just have sex with girls like all of my friends were. *So I obviously wasn't worried about being sexually moral. I just wanted to be sexually normal.*
>
> My desire to be made straight was all about me. I had no interest in being reconciled to God or having a relationship with Christ.[22]

Moore goes on to say that the root of his struggle wasn't homosexuality. That was just a symptom, albeit a powerful one. His heart needed to be mended. Even after it was, the struggle continued:

> Am I now straight? Am I now normal? Am I now free from same-sex desires and attracted solely to women?
>
> No, no and no.
>
> My heart was changed instantaneously when I trusted in Christ and began to follow Him, but my mind was not. I now have a heart that genuinely loves God and desires to worship Him, but at the same time, I'm still utterly messed up and damaged by sin. The Lord is working in me and renewing my mind day by day, shaping me more and more into the reflection of Him that I was created to be. But it's

been a process. And it will continue to be a process until I receive a new, perfect and sinless body in the age to come. When that day comes, the fullness of what Jesus purchased for me will be given to me: full freedom from every sinful thing that restrains my enjoyment and worship of God.[23]

There's a strange comfort in that, isn't there? Those in the LGBT community haven't found completeness despite the legalization of same-sex marriage in the Netherlands, United States, and Canada. Those with gender dysphoria typically find everything except peace even after sex reassignment surgery. Those who struggle with temptations for other unbiblical fulfillments don't find satisfaction by indulging those temptations. In that sense, all of us are dysphoric. Our identities have been marred since the fall of Adam and Eve. The congruence between our souls and our bodies was jolted out of alignment because the congruence of our relationship with God was jolted out of alignment. Adam and Eve suddenly perceived their nakedness. What was once harmonious and pure was suddenly discordant and shameful. Lack of clothing wasn't the root of their shame. Lack of harmony with God was. We may not act or even feel perfect once we give our lives to Christ. But we are given a coping mechanism that leads us out of the despair. Paul says to us, "Walk by the Spirit, and you will not gratify the desires of the flesh" (Galatians 5:16). What's interesting is that he doesn't say, "You will not *have* the desires of the flesh." He says that we will no longer be slaves to such desires. To return to Jesus' words: The Son will set us free and we will be free indeed.

There's a liberty there that's terribly ironic, isn't there?

When we exercise unfettered autonomy, we lose sight of our sacredness and become prisoners to our own freedoms. But when we find our true identity in Christ, we bind ourselves to his Lordship and find a liberating means to become who we were made to be.

I truly feel that we can learn much from those who struggle with gender dysphoria or who experience sexual attractions beyond the Bible's boundaries, yet have looked to Jesus to find wholeness. Their agony of being in two places at once may remain, but their hope and devotion to Christ gets stronger. For them, the painful discord may yield surprising meaningfulness because the cross of Christ resonates in harmony with their pain. I think of an amazing statement made by one of Mark Yarhouse's friends, a Christian who still suffers through her gender incongruence:

> Suffering in Christianity is not only not meaningless, it is ultimately one of the most powerful media for the transmission of meaning. We can stand in adoration between the cross, and kneel and kiss the wood that bore the body of our Saviour, because this is the means by which the ugly meaningless atheistic suffering of the world (the problem of evil) was transmuted into the living water, the blood of Christ, the wellspring of Creation. The great paradox here is that the Tree of Death and Suffering is the Tree of Life. This central paradox in Christianity allows us to love our own brokenness precisely because it is through that brokenness that we image the broken body of our God—and the highest expression of divine love. That God in some sense wills it to be so seems evident in Gethsemane: Christ prays "Not

my will, but thine be done," and when God's will is done
it involves the scourge and the nails. It's also always struck
me as particularly fitting and beautiful that when Christ is
resurrected His body is not returned to a state of perfection,
as the body of Adam in Eden, but rather it still bares the
marks of His suffering and death—and indeed it is precisely
through these marks that He is known by Thomas.[24]

Her words are worth quoting a thousand times. She captures the
paradox of Christianity—that we have a new identity in Christ,
but we don't always get magically cleared up. When Christians
suffer, they do so in solidarity with Christ. We struggle together
in a community of brokenness. There, we all can be understood.
Our shared hope is in a Savior whose body was broken for us.

Emily Brontë's poem "The Prisoner" comes to mind.
The jailer and an unnamed observer mock the Prisoner. But
the Prisoner finds her sacred identity in seeing her need for
redemption, having seen her former life without it as the true
prison. There is that moment of agony when she recognizes
that she has given up her former life. But there is bliss in finding her true self:

> Oh dreadful is the check—intense the agony—
> When the ear begins to hear, and the eye begins to see;
> When the pulse begins to throb, the brain to think again;
> The soul to feel the flesh, and the flesh to feel the chain.
> Yet I would lose no sting, would wish no torture less;
> The more that anguish racks, the earlier it will bless;
> And robed in fires of hell, or bright with heavenly shine,
> If it but herald death, the vision is divine!

She is no longer the Prisoner because Christ has freed her soul. It is the jailer, and even the unnamed mocker, who remain imprisoned. Realizing that the Prisoner's sacred freedom has transcended her physical cell, the mocker realizes:

> She ceased to speak, and we, unanswering, turned
>   to go—
> We had no further power to work the captive woe:
> Her cheek, her gleaming eye, declared that man had
>   given
> A sentence, unapproved, and overruled by Heaven.[25]

Brontë's Prisoner had to feel the agony before the redemption that revealed her sacred identity would come. But come it did.

Only the Lord of glory can sum up all of this in but one statement: "Whoever loses his life for my sake will find it" (Matthew 16:25). As I bring this chapter to a close, I'm reminded of Jesus' encounter with the lame man near the Pool of Bethesda in the Gospel of John. In chapter 5 we read that every Sabbath day, the man had struggled with all of his strength to plunge himself into the pool's healing waters, only to be beaten to it by the swift-footed crowd. On a particular Sabbath day, he encountered Jesus. But Jesus didn't help the man into the pool. He healed the man's legs. Jesus told the rejoicing man to take up the mat he had been sitting on all those Sabbath days. Strangely, the pious Pharisees criticized the man for lifting the mat—for working on the Sabbath day of rest. The new identity the man had in his Messiah was totally lost on them. They failed to realize that Jesus freed the man to finally enjoy a true Sabbath rest in the grace of God.

We struggle to break ourselves free of the flesh's chains or to plunge ourselves in the healing waters. We think we can do it by exercising our autonomy or rebelling against God's boundaries of gender and sexuality. But when we give ourselves to Christ, we realize that we have been understood all along. The agony may be intense but after it comes sacred Sabbath rest.

CHAPTER 7

Clarity about Science and Faith

A humorous story is told of a man walking down a street who sees a sign in a travel agency's window that reads, "River Cruise! Only $100!" Amazed at the incredible deal, he strides into the storefront, plunks down a crisp $100 bill and says to the woman behind the counter, "Sign me up!"

He's suddenly struck on the head from behind.

He regains consciousness only to find himself crammed into a barrel, bobbing down a river. He looks to his right and sees another man rubbing the back of his own head, also floating down the river in a barrel. Perplexed, he yells, "Hey! Do they serve lunch on this cruise?"

The other man shouts back, "Well, they didn't last year!"

Some believe that religious people are like the second man, gullibly clinging to wishful thinking despite having evidence to the contrary. In his book *The God Delusion*, Richard Dawkins writes, "A delusion is a persistent false belief held in the face of strong contradictory evidence, especially as a symptom of psychiatric disorder. . . . God is . . . a delusion and a pernicious delusion. . . . When one person suffers from a delusion, it is called insanity. When many people suffer from a delusion it is called Religion."[1]

The dangerous delusion of religion, some believe, can only be cured by the benevolent panacea of science. "Science flies you to the moon," Victor Stenger is credited as quipping, "but religion flies you into buildings."

As cleverly worded as that aphorism is, it's rife with over-generalization and confusion. Take, for example, the confusion in his statement "Science flies you to the moon." In common parlance, we talk as if science were a benevolent, conscious entity that tells us how the world works and bestows gifts on us like vaccines and iPhones. We say things like, "According to science, humans have evolved from simpler life forms," or "Science tells us where love is in the brain," and the like. But science is only a method of observing, measuring, and making predictions about the physical world. It has no volition of its own with which to act, no voice of its own with which to speak, and no conscience with which to judge. Put simply, *science doesn't say anything. Scientists* say things based on the conclusions they reach, sometimes through a scientific method. And yes, like the rest of us, scientists have their own biases to deal with.

This inaccurate anthropomorphism of science isn't just semantics, it's a leading cause of the confusion about how science and faith interact. This is critical for us to understand because confusion about both science and religion creates false narratives of opposition. While we often credit science with the world's wonderful advancements, we blame religion for all of society's ills. But if science actually "says" or "does" things, like fly us to the moon, then why can't we just as easily lay at science's feet all the ills of the world too? If science flew us to the moon, then science also irradiated Hiroshima and Nagasaki and gave us mustard gas and eugenics. Sure, a naturalistic atheist might counter by saying that science is merely a method that people have used and abused for their own ends. Could one not, in turn, offer the same defense of religion? But religion, a naturalist might retort, is a set of commands compelling people to do heinous acts to each other, whereas science is merely a method of study that doesn't compel us to act one way or another. The naturalist thus proves the point: science is merely a method after all. Therefore Stenger's statement, however cleverly stated, is quite meaningless.

To say that "religion" is a set of commands that compel actions, good or bad, is an oversimplification. Influential religions like Buddhism and Confucianism don't even posit the existence of a God from which such commands emanate. Further, the idea that "religion" is a set of commands isn't necessarily a bad thing. Politics, law, and ethics are all governed by sets of commands. Religion often gives these commands a divine authority and imposes an obligation. If we take irreligion or mere reason to be our authorities, however, there are still commands we submit ourselves to. The problem is that they lack any objective basis beyond opinion. And if there is no God, then the set of commands is just the law of the jungle. Saying that religion is a set of commands doesn't get naturalism off any philosophical or ethical hooks.

Further, religion is more like science than some might wish to acknowledge. While usually including rules and commands, religion is also a method for making sense of the world. In fact, it can be a much broader method than science. Many religions seek to give us an understanding of not only the physical world but also the nonphysical world. Many religions, like Christianity, embrace science as a means to understand the natural part of the larger reality while also embracing philosophy, theology, and other means of exploring the non-physical parts of reality.

The current confusion over science and faith is made even worse by our misuse of the word *faith*. Many of us, including some religious believers, define faith as blind belief or belief where there is no evidence. This pits faith and science against each other by implying that the more we learn through the empirical sciences, the less we need faith. Other religions may define faith this way, but it is an utterly unbiblical understanding of faith. That's why I don't intend here to argue for the harmony of science and *religion* in general. What I intend to do is clear up the confusion that surrounds the interaction of science and the Christian faith. It's my contention that the Christian faith and the findings of science (in fact the very enterprise of science itself) are harmonious. I'll leave other religions to defend themselves.

Have Science and Faith Been at Odds through History?

I remember my elementary school days learning about the Copernican Revolution. Nicholas Copernicus debunked the then commonly held belief that the sun revolves around the earth by showing that the opposite is true. What stands out most about that lesson, however, was the "church versus science" narrative. We were taught—as so many were and have been—that the Roman

Catholic Church sought to quell Copernicus's revolution by jailing one of its champions, the prominent scientist Galileo Galilei. That story sent quite the clear message: Christians have been afraid of science because it undermines the church's authority and erodes belief in God.

This narrative of conflict between the church and the scientific community has persisted ever since Galileo's day. Some think that religion is inherently the enemy of scientific progress and that we would all benefit from religion's demise. Others, like the late Stephen Jay Gould, have been a bit more circumspect, viewing religion and science as "Non-Overlapping Magisteria." According to Gould, religion has its place in helping us to find subjective meaning or morality, but it's science that provides us with objective facts about the natural world. In either view, a dichotomy has been set up: Religion (or matters of spiritual faith) has nothing to do with the real world. Objective, verifiable truth is science's sole purview. So let's not fool ourselves into thinking that faith in God can benefit our scientific pursuits.

This is historically and philosophically false. People of faith, particularly the Christian faith, have been at the forefront of scientific discoveries for much of the modern era (and even before that). It was Catholics and Protestants who founded the most famous and influential academic institutions in the world, from Oxford to Harvard to Yale to the University of Notre Dame. True, those institutions have become more secularized in our day, but let's not forget that Oxford's motto comes from the opening line of Psalm 27: *Dominus Illuminatio Mea*, "The Lord is my light." Oxford's founders believed that God's endowment of rational thought would illuminate our academic pursuits. Copernicus himself—the progenitor of the Copernican Revolution—was a Christian. Scientific luminaries of both older and more recent vintages have been Christians: Tycho Brahe, Gregor Mendel, Johannes Kepler, Blaise Pascal, Robert Boyle, Michael Faraday, Francis Bacon, Louis Pasteur, James Clerk Maxwell, and the incomparable Isaac Newton, to name a few. Contemporary thinkers and scientists find no incongruity between their faith in the God of the Bible and their scientific pursuits. Such a list includes the likes of Francis Collins (world-famous geneticist), John Lennox (three doctorates, including one in mathematics from Oxford), Hugh Ross (doctorate in astronomy from Cal Tech), James Tour (doctorate in chemistry and professor at Rice University), Ian Hutchinson (professor of nuclear science at MIT), Ard Louis (Oxford professor of theoretical physics), John Polkinghorne (professor of physics at Cambridge), and Kenneth Miller (biology professor at Brown University).

This list barely qualifies as incomplete, as there are far more scientists who believe in God than many might think. Edward Larson and Larry Witham's 1996 survey revealed that 40 percent of the working scientists they surveyed believe in a God who answers prayer.[2] While that's not quite half, it is a significant number given the commonly held beliefs that almost no serious scientists believe in God and that a serious pursuit of science will knock the faith out of a person. Some have retorted that scientists who believe typically exchange their Bibles for lab coats when they do their work. And yet I know some of the people named above and can attest that it is their belief in God that drives them to do good science. Isaac Newton, arguably one of the most influential scientists in history, said in his masterwork *Opticks*:

> How came the Bodies of Animals to be contrived with so much Art, and for what ends were their several parts? Was the Eye contrived without Skill in Opticks, and the Ear without Knowledge of Sounds? . . . And these things being rightly dispatch'd, does it not appear from Phænomena that there is a Being incorporeal, living, intelligent . . . ?[3]

The idea that the world around us displays evidence of a transcendent mind fascinated and compelled Newton. Discovering what that transcendent mind did in creation was what drove people like him to pioneer new fields of science.

What then do we make of the oft-told story of Galileo's alleged persecution by the church for being a principled man of science? David Bentley Hart has addressed the oversimplified story, pointing out that Galileo's trial was more about how his inflated ego conflicted with other inflated personalities than it was about how science and Christianity conflicted. Contrary to the common narrative, Pope Urban VIII encouraged Galileo's work and Christian benefactors paid for Galileo's legal defense. But Galileo managed to offend and embarrass all the wrong people, especially certain figures with comparably inflated egos but incomparably inflated political power.[4]

Clarity about Science's Limits

Misconceptions about science are just as prevalent as those about faith. Contrary to common belief, there isn't something called *the* scientific method. Philosophers of science and scientists themselves acknowledge that there are different views on what science *is*. And different types of science employ different methodologies. Regardless of which method one ascribes to, the many different sciences have one thing in common: they help us to explore *the natural world*. Thus, by definition, science isn't equipped—or even meant—to study the nonphysical world. Science, therefore, is limited in its scope.

That statement might surprise some people and offend others. That's because perhaps the most pervasive misconception about science is that it is the sole means by which we know truth. We've been told science is a universal solvent that dissolves all the big questions of life. *How do humans think?* Science will tell us. *What explains love?* Science can answer. *Where did we come from?* Ask science. But turning to science for the answers to these questions isn't science. It's *scientism*. Scientism is the view that science is either the only or most reliable way to know the truth about the real world. It's proponents usually discount philosophy, literature, and other fields in the humanities as truth revealing. Science is the best, and sometimes the only, game in town.

When defenders of scientism get exercised over the claim that science isn't sufficient to answer all important questions, it's quite fascinating. We've heard time and again how science is the dispassionate pursuit of truth. But the minute someone points out that science has built-in limitations, dispassionate scholars become quite inflamed with all the passion of a zealot. Darwinian evolution's high priest, Richard Dawkins, has said that anyone who denies evolution is ignorant, stupid, or insane. He sounds very much like a fundamentalist. Michael Ruse, an atheist philosopher who specializes in evolution, forthrightly calls out the new scientism, particularly evolutionary scientism, for being a religious belief. "I am an ardent evolutionist and an ex-Christian," Ruse says. "But I must admit that in this one complaint . . . the literalists are absolutely right. Evolution is a religion. This was true of evolution in the beginning and it is true of evolution still today."[5]

Blindness about scientism's religiosity underlies the confusion about the relationship between science and faith. Out of the right side of their mouths naturalistic atheists protest that science isn't a religious belief, that it's only a method for observing and making predictions about the physical world. Out of the left side, they argue that we ought to use only science to tell us about morality, meaning, love, and human purpose. David Berlinski, a secular agnostic Jew, hits the mark in observing that "from cosmology to biology, [science's] narratives have become the narratives. They are, these narratives, immensely seductive, so much so that looking at them with innocent eyes requires a very deliberate act. And like any militant church, this one places a familiar demand before all others: Thou shalt have no other gods before me."[6]

Only one side of the mouth is right: science isn't a religion. Therefore, it has a very narrow explanatory scope. Scientism, on the other hand, is a set of commands after all and so looks a lot like the religion that naturalists decry.

Further, to embrace scientism is to embrace illogic. David Hume, the brilliant Scottish skeptic, articulated the idea that science is the sole method for understanding truth and therefore everything else is mere speculative sophistry. To summarize Hume, if a claim or idea can't be measured, experimented on, or mathematically proven, we ought to "Commit it then to the flame; for it can contain nothing but sophistry and illusion."[7] Despite his brilliance, Hume made a colossal error because his very argument can't be measured, experimented upon, or mathematically proven. And so Hume would have to commit his own argument to the flames. How fascinating that such a brilliant man stoked a furnace that would consume his own philosophy.

Indeed, the self-contradiction runs even deeper. If, as some scientists claim, we are just neurochemical machines that respond to stimuli, then we don't actually use reason to reach scientific conclusions. In fact, we aren't endowed with reason at all, we are just capable of mechanistic reactions. With far more rigor than I can flesh out here, Philosopher Alvin Plantinga brilliantly points out that belief in God isn't the enemy of science—naturalistic evolutionary atheism is. He explains that naturalistic evolution entails that our beliefs aren't based on whether they're true, but on how they help us survive and propagate our species. Thus, the truth or falsity of our beliefs, including those derived through science, is irrelevant. But science is supposed to be about the pursuit of truth. And if truth doesn't matter in atheistic evolution, then science isn't even possible.[8] Thus, we can't scientifically prove or rationally conclude that evolution actually happened. Thomas Nagel, whom I've mentioned previously, agrees: "Evolutionary naturalism implies that we shouldn't take any of our convictions seriously, including the scientific world picture on which evolutionary naturalism itself depends."[9]

Hard sciences aren't broad enough to help us unlock all of life's mysteries. We need history to learn lessons about our past failures and successes. Literature and poetry inspire us and make us self-reflective. Philosophy helps us explore logic. Good religion takes all of those fields and combines them with revelation to tell us who we are, why we're here, and where we're going. Science intentionally focuses on the universe's mechanistic workings. Thus, limiting ourselves to science forces us to look at the wider panorama of reality through a narrow keyhole. To switch metaphors, David Bentley Hart points out that "some things are more easily seen through a red filter, but to go through life wearing rose colored spectacles is not to see things as they truly are."[10] Science, like the filter, can help us see aspects of the physical world that were once unseen. But if we only look at the world through science's filter, we will rob ourselves of a broader view.

Mistaking science's keyhole for the panoramic window has important moral implications. If scientific naturalism reduces us to complex chemical machines or sophisticated chimps, it follows that there really is no moral dimension to human existence. I've written in more detail about this elsewhere, but suffice it to say here that a good number of atheists actually agree that if there is no God, if the natural or physical world is all there is, then there is no morality.[11] A world devoid of objective morality collides with our heightened concern about racial and gender equality. If we're just chemical machines, we're obviously quite different machines. Some of us are stronger, faster, or smarter than others. Indeed, the mechanism that drives Darwinian evolution—natural selection—operates on the idea that the stronger, faster, and smarter members of a species will eventually outcompete other members to achieve genetic success.

We have to be careful here. We mustn't say that those who ascribe to Darwinian evolution are necessarily racist or genocidal. That's far too broad a brush with which to paint. It would be unfair to do so. In *The Descent of Man*, however, Darwin himself expressed concern over the social impact his theory might have (please pardon some of the offensive outdated terms):

> With savages, the weak in body or mind are soon eliminated; and those that survive commonly exhibit a vigorous state of health. We civilized men, on the other hand, do our utmost to check the process of elimination. We build asylums for the imbecile, the maimed and the sick; we institute poor-laws; and our medical men exert their utmost skill to save the life of every one to the last moment. . . . Thus the weak members of civilized societies propagate their kind. No one who has attended to the breeding of domestic animals will doubt that his must be highly injurious to the race of man.[12]

As Darwinism spilled over the brim of the biological sciences and into the cups of social sciences, atrocities were just around the corner. Darwinian evolution didn't directly cause Hitler's final solution, but it did allow him to justify it. As historian Richard Weikart wrote, "Darwinism by itself did not produce the Holocaust, but without Darwinism, especially in its social Darwinist and eugenics permutations, neither Hitler nor his Nazi followers would have the necessary scientific underpinning to convince themselves and their collaborators that one of the world's greatest atrocities was really morally praiseworthy."[13]

Again, caution is in order. We dare not denigrate the gift that science (and scientists) have been to humanity. Through science we have made wonderful discoveries like penicillin, tectonic plates, and planetary bodies. We've invented airplanes, cars, and even the computer I'm typing on. But we need more than naturalistic sciences. We cannot derive meaning, human value, and equality from a laboratory. The vast majority of those who ascribe to Darwinian evolution—be they atheists, agnostics, or religious believers—find racism, genocide, sexism, and the like morally repugnant. Just as religious people wince in revulsion when religion is used to justify such evils, so naturalists wince when evolution is used to do the same. The confusion comes when we claim that science is the sole means of understanding the world. A worldview based solely on science's limitations can lead us to a world devoid of equality. And yet we continue to strive for that equality. Clarity comes when we acknowledge the transcendent, nonphysical source for the nonphysical phenomenon of morality.

Clarity about Faith

A man approached me just as I finished a dialogue with atheist speaker Red McCall at West Texas A&M University on the topic "The Good Life: What My Worldview Means to Me." The man from the audience asked me, "Abdu, why do you think faith provides a valid epistemological basis?" It was a fancily worded way to ask, "Why do you think faith is a valid way of knowing things?" He had gotten that question from a book called A *Manual for Creating Atheists* by Peter Boghossian. Because I also had read that book, I knew where he wanted to take the conversation. "I don't think faith is a way of knowing things about the world," I responded. "I think you may have made a category mistake. Faith isn't the way we know things. Biblical faith means *trust*. The evidence that I do know through reason and my senses points me to trust God." I suspect he didn't like that answer because it didn't fit the script offered by Boghossian's *Manual*. "No, that's not the definition of faith," he retorted. "The Bible equates faith and evidence. Doesn't it say somewhere that 'faith is evidence of things you don't know' or something like that?"

He was trying to quote Hebrews 11:1 from the King James translation, which says, "Faith is the substance of things hoped for, the evidence of things not seen." Other translations more accurately render the passage, "Now faith is the assurance of things hoped for, the conviction of things not seen" (ESV, see also NASB, NIV, and NRSV for nearly identical translations). While we often use faith and hope synonymously, Hebrews 11:1 shows that they aren't synonyms. *Hope* is a positive expectation of a desired future event. *Faith* is trusting in the one who promised to make that event happen. In fact, the Greek word translated as *faith* is *pistis*, which means *trust*. And, as is usually the case, simply reading the context of a biblical passage explains more of the meaning. Hebrews 11:1 says that faith is our assurance and conviction of the things we do not see. Seeing is one way to observe evidence, but it isn't the only way. Hebrews 11:3 then says, "By faith we understand that the universe was created by the word of God, so that what is seen was not made out of things that are visible." We use reason to infer that the cause of what is visible is invisible. In other words, faith is not blind even when we cannot see. We see the evidence of the physical world around us, and this allows us to reasonably infer that it must have come from a nonphysical, unseeable source. And it is by faith—trust—that we understand God to be that source.

That's exactly what Big Bang cosmology implies. The standard cosmological model states that time and the material universe came into being from a nonmaterial state of nothingness at a finite point in the past. In other words, the universe isn't eternal and everything sprung from nothing. And because nothing does, well, nothing, the universe couldn't have created itself. Something nontemporal and nonmaterial must have created time and the material world. That is the logical inference from the scientific evidence that we have. Thus, just as Hebrews 11:1–3 suggests, we have reason to trust that the universe that we *can* see was created by something we *cannot* see.

Until relatively recently, scientists believed that the universe was eternal. Einstein's general theory of relativity and Edwin Hubble's discovery that celestial bodies are moving away from each other showed that the cosmos had a beginning. The opening verse of the Bible also asserts that the universe had a beginning: "In the beginning, God created the heavens and the earth" (Genesis 1:1). The writer of Hebrews didn't have Einstein's theories or Hubble's discoveries to prove that the world was created by the unseen. The writer trusted Genesis's millennia-old account because of the evidence of design all around him. Robert Jastrow remarked that scientists climbed the mountain of cosmological knowledge only to find a group of theologians who had been there for centuries.

The fact is, everyone has a faith of some kind. Without it, life would be unlivable. If we only acted based on absolute certainty of knowledge, we could never actually do anything. When you drive to work, you don't test your brakes to make certain that they won't fail and plunge you into a fiery car wreck. You trust the brakes. But that trust isn't blind. You have enough evidence that brakes tend not to fail without warning to warrant getting into your car without going through a multi-point inspection. Of course, we've all seen stories of brakes failing without warning. And yet we still get into our cars, thousands of times a year, putting our lives at risk based on our faith in auto parts. We similarly trust doctors with our health even though we have no real way of knowing if they are correctly diagnosing us. And when a person believes that science proves this or that theory, she has faith that the scientists who conducted the experiments or reported the findings did so competently and honestly. Faith is a part of every worldview.

We come to know things through our senses and by applying our reasoning and wisdom. We have faith based on what we know, however incomplete our knowledge may be. This is what Hebrews 11:1–3 means when it says that "by faith we understand." I trust my wife's fidelity because of years of proof of her integrity even though I don't know what she's doing all the time or where she might be at every moment. I have *faith* in her because I *know* she's trustworthy. And so the question isn't whether we have faith. The question is whether the one in whom our faith is placed is worthy of it.

Is God Worthy of Our Faith?

Still, one might ask, shouldn't belief in God be different? If what we believe about God determines our ultimate destiny, shouldn't the evidence be more obvious and available? If knowing God is so important, why does he remain so hidden? Space doesn't permit us to explore all the answers to these questions here, but allow me to address two ways in which God's supposed hiddenness reveals something profound about us and about God's character.

First, our demands for obvious and undeniable evidence reveals quite a bit about our attitudes toward evidence. What qualifies, exactly, as "undeniable" evidence for God's existence? A giant golden cross in the sky greeting us every morning would do the trick, some would say. Or seeing an eye grow back in its socket after prayer—that might suffice. But is there such a thing as undeniable evidence no matter what subject we're examining? Or do we find ways to deny strong evidence when it challenges our perspectives or desires?

I've often thought of the phenomenon of smoking. The evidence that smoking causes cancer and is addictive is overwhelming. And yet each of us knows (or is) someone who knew that evidence and chose to start smoking anyway. Undeniable evidence, it seems, doesn't always matter after all. In fact, intelligent and informed people are quite willing to put their lives at risk despite knowing the evidence. Sometimes we tailor our beliefs and actions to fit the evidence. And sometimes we tailor the evidence (or ignore it altogether) to fit our beliefs and actions. Blaise Pascal said that God has provided enough evidence in this world to make belief in him quite reasonable, but he has withheld enough evidence to make belief in him without faith impossible. The fact that we ignore that evidence says more about us than it does about God.

Second, the fact that God hasn't spoon-fed us all the answers reveals something wonderful about his character. God has orchestrated the universe and our existence to foster a sense of wonder. He has given us the pleasure of pursuing our wonder through discovering things that aren't so obvious. When my son was very young, he showed a fascination with letters and numbers. My wife and I responded to his affinity in typical first-time parents fashion: we bought him nearly every letter and number toy we could find. One was a Spider-Man laptop (really a simple speak-and-spell disguised as a laptop to fool toddlers into thinking they have a computer). It displayed letters so he could memorize their sounds and short words to eventually read. With his "laptop" open, he sat at the kitchen table with me and my wife. As Nicole and I talked, my attention was diverted when I heard a short word emerge from my son's mouth. "Ffffaaatt," he said. I turned to look at the screen and sure enough, it displayed the letters F-A-T. "I think he just read something!" I exclaimed to Nicole. I hit the "next" button and three more letters appeared: C-A-T. "C-C-Caaat," my son said. I must have pressed that next button a dozen more times, looking for three-letter words that rhymed with *fat*.

I was beaming. My wife was beaming. My son was squealing with the kind of delight that comes when a child "gets it." But Nicole and I were rapturous. Any parent reading this knows what it is to revel in their child's discoveries even more than the child does. This is what we read in the Bible about how God reacts to our discoveries:

> It is the glory of God to conceal things, but the glory of kings is to search things out. (Prov. 25:2)

God has concealed things in this world so that we can experience the glory and delight of discovery. Perfect solar eclipses illustrate this so well. Our moon "happens" to be exactly four hundred times smaller in diameter than our sun. And our sun "happens" to be exactly four hundred times farther from us than our moon. This allows for perfect solar eclipses in which the disk of the moon perfectly conceals the disk of the sun. During that concealment, aspects of the sun's corona become visible, allowing us to learn more about the corona, the sun's atmosphere, and solar flares.[14] In fact, perfect solar eclipses have allowed us to confirm Einstein's theory of general relativity, including his conclusion that massive gravitational objects like our sun bend space, which in turn "bends" light. During a perfect solar eclipse in 1919, astronomers measured the light from distant stars located in the line of sight just outside our sun (but aren't visible under normal conditions due to the sun's brightness) and confirmed that the light did in fact "bend" around the sun.[15]

This is a kind of fulfillment of Proverbs 25:2. God in his sovereignty has perfectly concealed the sun with the moon so that we can discover things about the universe. Is that not evidence that God not only sows within us the desire to explore but also feeds us with opportunities to fulfill that desire? That's the glory of kings in searching things out. The glory of God in concealing things is his rejoicing over our discoveries just as a parent rejoices over a child's learning.

Science and the Signals of Transcendence

The late sociologist Peter Berger coined a crystalline-sounding phrase about the small hints in life that point us to God. He called these hints *signals of transcendence*. Although science is a limited tool by which we explore the natural or physical world, what we learn through science has implications for our understanding of the supernatural. In other words, science, when used as a tool for the search for truth, can reveal signals of transcendence.

What signals can we see? The first is that anything in the cosmos is observable at all. Our solar system's placement within the Milky Way Galaxy gives us the optimum ability to view and explore the universe. If our solar system were placed elsewhere, the night sky would be filled with bright objects that would block our view.[16]

Indeed, that anything material even exists at all is itself a signal of transcendence. Gottfried Wilhelm Leibniz developed an argument for God's existence that goes something like this: All things that exist are either contingent (their existence is explained by something else) or noncontingent (they explain their own existence). An easy way to think of this is to see contingent things as things that didn't have to exist. It was possible for them not to have existed. Most things fit this description. It is possible that computers couldn't have existed. It's possible that I couldn't have existed (say, if my parents had never met). The universe is also a contingent thing. The universe is made up of particles. We can easily imagine there being less of those particles in the universe. If it's possible that some of the particles in the universe couldn't have existed, then it's possible that none of them could have existed. That makes the universe contingent and in need of an explanation for its existence. The explanation for all material contingent things has to be noncontingent—it must explain its own existence. And since the contingent material universe exists, its existence must be explained by an immaterial noncontingent being. The Bible describes God as the noncontingent being—the One in whom "we live and move and have our being" (Acts 17:28).[17]

Not only does the fact *that* the universe exists point to a transcendent source, but *how* the universe has been arranged points to a transcendent mind. The universe, especially in its initial conditions, is finely tuned to allow for life. This isn't a matter of controversy, as theists and atheists alike acknowledge that the conditions and forces at the universe's beginning fall within an exquisitely narrow, or fine, range to allow for life to develop. If any one of a number of those conditions and forces were even infinitesimally slightly different, life in the universe would be impossible. Oxford University's Roger Penrose gives us one example by calculating that the odds of the Big Bang's low entropy condition existing by chance are one out of $10^{10(123)}$. The denominator in that fraction would be impossible to write out in zeroes even if we could mark a zero on every atom in the universe. There are at least fifty such quantities and constants present in the Big Bang that must be similarly fine-tuned to permit life in the universe.

This kind of fine-tuning leads brilliant scientists like Paul Davies to believe that "a common reaction among physicists to remarkable discoveries . . . is a mixture of delight at the subtlety and elegance of nature, and of stupefaction." This leads him to ask, "If nature is so 'clever' it can exploit mechanisms that amaze us with their ingenuity, is that not persuasive evidence for the existence of intelligent design behind the physical universe?"[18] Davies says that discoveries about the universe lead to delight. He may as well have quoted Proverbs 25:2.[19]

It isn't only outer space that points to design but also inner space. Using biomimetics, scientists solve human engineering problems by mimicking the structures and functions of biological organisms (even single-cell organisms). Through bioinspiration, we literally draw motivation for our designs from the inherent design efficiencies in nature. And even when we try to imitate life's sophistication, we come up short of the Creator's magnificence. A few years ago, computer scientists from Japan and Germany were able to simulate one second of human brain activity through computers. But to do it, they had to connect 82,944 processors to one of the most powerful mainframes in the world. And even then, the vast array of processors took forty minutes to simulate what your brain and my brain are capable of doing in just one second.[20] In other words, our brains are 2,400 times faster than the best computers our finest minds can assemble. Biomimetics and bioinspiration cause us to ask of biology what Davies asked about the universe: *How could blind, mindless nature outwit humanity's finest engineering minds?* To ask the question is to answer it.

Only now, with our high-powered microscopes, are we able to see the engineering marvels all around us that were once hidden from our view. Once again, God in his glory has concealed things so that we can delight in finding them. I first learned about biomimetics from Dr. Fazale Rana, a biochemist out of Ohio University now working with a group of scientists called Reasons to Believe.[21] He pointed to the hints within the Bible that direct us to draw inspiration from biological organisms:

> But ask the beasts, and they will teach you; the birds of the heavens, and they will tell you; or the bushes of the earth, and they will teach you; and the fish of the sea will declare to you. Who among all these does not know that the hand of the LORD has done this? (Job 12:7–9)

By copying biological systems to solve our design problems, we are exercising faith in life's Designer so that we can do better science. To call that ironic is an understatement.

This takes us beyond irony and into poetry. It's been said that art imitates life. Through biomimetics, we've come to the point that science imitates life too. The poetry is that only God explains how the human mind can be capable of artistry and science. And we've used those God-given abilities to see God's artistic designs throughout the very universe he created for us to explore.

The intricate weaving of DNA provides another signal of transcendence. Francis Crick, himself a committed atheist, acknowledged that "the origin of life appears at the moment to be almost a miracle, so many are the conditions which would have had to have been satisfied to get it going."[22] And yet he had to warn scientists that the appearance of design in biological and biochemical systems is so compelling that they have to constantly remind themselves that what they are looking at isn't designed.[23] That's quite a tacit admission of the powerful inferences we can draw from the appearance of biological design.

A Sea of Glass, Mingled with Fire

The essayist F. W. Boreham wonderfully explores how seemingly contrary things mingle together to give us a comprehensive picture. Boreham tells the story of a young girl who called an ocean sunset "a sea of glass, mingled with fire." The contrarieties of water and fire coming together beautifully describes the truth behind what a sunset actually is. The sea glistens with the glassy reflections of the sun's fire. What a beautiful way to describe a phenomenon that is paradoxically simple and complex.

Boreham goes on to say that science and faith interact similarly.[24] While they are seemingly contradictory, they are mutually complimentary. Together, they give us a clearer picture of the simplicity and complexity of the world around us. One only needs to see a picture of DNA's 3.1 billion bits of information complexly woven together to see why Crick was so worried about the implication of design. The complexity of DNA revealed to us through science underscores a simple truth given to us in Scripture. The Bible doesn't say that we are built, manufactured, or even designed. It describes our creation in a much more intimate way:

> For you formed my inward parts; you *knitted* me together
> in my mother's womb. (Psalm 139:13, emphasis mine)

When we read that word—*knitted*—the image appears of a maternal figure sitting in a chair, lovingly weaving together a blanket or sweater. When she was pregnant with me, my mother knitted a little purple sweater to bring me home from the hospital in. I've kept that sweater, and my wife and I have wrapped each of our kids in it for the journey home after their births. As my mother wove those threads together, I was on her mind. That kind of intimacy soaks God's description of how He created each one of us. Science alone cannot tell us why we're here. Science alone—with the philosophical assumption of naturalistic atheism—leads someone like Lawrence Krauss to call us "cosmic pollution" that is "completely irrelevant." But when coupled with a larger worldview that allows for nature's design to speak to us about ultimate purpose, science can lead us to see that we are significant and relevant not only to each other but also to the One who created it all. Science confirms the truths in Scripture. Scripture unveils the poetry of science. The confusing fog of the false dichotomy between science and faith fades. The sea of glass mingled with fire that is the intertwining of faith and science becomes clear. The signals of transcendence reveal our relevance to the Transcendent One.

CHAPTER 8

Clarity about Religious Pluralism

The *ohm* charm on her necklace signaled her beliefs before she spoke to me. And when she did speak, she surprised me by doing so in Arabic. Both her religious beliefs and her use of language were surprising because she was clearly Western. She learned Arabic from her Lebanese husband (who had just introduced us) and learned Hinduism from studying the popular Eastern mystics. She further surprised me by referring to the poetry and essays of Khalil Gibran, the famous Lebanese poet. Gibran believed in God but was a universalist who eloquently rebelled against the divisiveness he thought lay at the heart of organized religion. Her husband was a devoted Christian. She was a dedicated pantheist. It wasn't surprising that we ended up discussing religious pluralism and her objections to the Christian claim that only one path leads to God.

Her main point of contention with me was on the role of personal experience in religious belief versus the role of logic in choosing a faith. "Where we differ," she said, "is that you think logic excludes certain faiths from being true paths to God, while I believe that each of our experiences of God shows us that we're all on the right path." She was echoing a very popular and well-meaning sentiment—one that's frequently recited over the Culture of Confusion's loudspeakers.

She explained to me that according to Hinduism, all of us are paying off our karma from previous lives, and whatever religious path we choose may help us to pay off our karma on the way to achieving oneness with the sole creative force of the universe. "So," she concluded, "I can affirm that Christianity is the path for you, even if it isn't the path for me. We don't need to say one view is right and the other is wrong."

"But you believe that you are on the path toward realizing your oneness with God, right?" I asked. "Jesus claimed to be the only way to God. And he specifically said that our destiny is not to be God, but to dwell with God. So how can you possibly say Christianity is a valid path if it contradicts your views?"

Her response was fascinating. "I know this is true because Jesus came to me in a dream and told me that I'm on the right path with Hinduism and that all people are on the path to ultimate unity with the divine." That immediately took our conversation in a new direction. Hindus and Muslims the world over report that they converted to Christianity in part because Jesus came to them in a dream or vision and told them that he is the Son of God and the only path to salvation. So I asked her about those. "Why is your dream of Jesus more valid than theirs?"

The point I was hoping to make is that she was being just as exclusive in her claims as I was. In her effort to be religiously inclusive, she excluded the religious exclusivists. Failure to recognize that all views are exclusive at some level is at the heart of the culture's confusion about religious pluralism. Pluralism was once a clear idea. It meant that all religious and nonreligious worldviews were welcome to set up their booths in the marketplace of ideas where we could debate their merits. Today, pluralism is an amorphous concept that confusingly uses "tolerance" to shield certain religions from scrutiny and assail other religions for having the temerity of believing that they're actually true.

Recovering clarity about pluralism is critical if we're to truly understand and respect each other. My intention here isn't to delve into all of the detailed differences between the major religions. I've done that more extensively in my book *Grand Central Question* and others have gone even deeper.[1] Here I hope to offer clarity that (1) tolerance simply can't mean universal agreement with everyone's different beliefs, (2) only by recognizing their fundamental disagreements can we take different faith systems seriously and respectfully, and (3) believing that Jesus is the only way to God is a claim that is worth investigating.

Tolerant for You but Not for Me

Pluralism is a good thing, and religious pluralism is especially good. It allows us to explore different claims about the most important questions of life, like purpose, meaning, and destiny. We used to be able to explore those claims in what Os Guinness calls the Civil Public Square. The problem today is that the public square isn't always very civil. In the past few decades, our religious rhetoric had become so heated that all we ever seemed to do is inflame each other's anger. We grew weary of the vitriol, so society underwent a pendular swing. To avoid hurting anyone's feelings, we decided that we can no longer scrutinize anyone's religious claims (well, almost anyone's).

Accordingly, we've shunned almost all religious debate. When someone makes a religious claim, we can't ask probing questions. We have to smile and nod with interest, lest we be branded intolerant. The cost of avoiding that stigma has been ignorance about the richness of the various religious traditions. That self-imposed ignorance gives birth to a confusion with many heads. We confuse engaging in argumentation with quarreling. We confuse disagreeing with someone's beliefs with disrespecting the person. In fact, we've confused the difference between people and ideas altogether. Where we once used to be able to challenge a person's beliefs without necessarily denigrating that person, we now think that challenging certain beliefs is the same thing as denigrating the person who holds them. As a Christian from a Muslim background, I find it fascinating that the Culture of Confusion speedily brands someone who criticizes Islam to be a "racist." Islam is a religion, not a race. People from many races and ethnicities embrace Islam. Calling someone a racist for criticizing Islam ignores Islam's racial and ethnic diversity. And so one could more justifiably call such a confused use of the term racist to be, well, racist itself. The Culture of Confusion waves tolerance around as carelessly as a toddler who's found his father's gun.

This mutation of pluralism is especially puzzling given that we don't seem to hold back on invective and criticism in other areas of life. Stephen Prothero points out that while no one argues that differing economic and political systems are essentially the same, religion enjoys a privileged status. "Scholars continue to claim that religious rivals such as Hinduism and

Islam, Judaism and Christianity are, by some miracle of the imagination, essentially the same," he writes. "And this view resounds in the echo chamber of popular culture, not least in Dan Brown's multi-million-dollar Da Vinci Code franchise."[2] We conjure up that miracle of the imagination from our preference to avoid doing the hard and uncomfortable work of honestly assessing what the world's most cherished views have to say. What's become more important is that we're seen as tolerant across the religious board. Personal preferences have dominated facts and truth yet again. Confusion about whether any particular religion is true has become a virtue. Clarity about the differences in religion—and that they can't all be right—has become a vice.

Confusion and the Roads to God

The Culture of Confusion's comforting mantras are easily identifiable. *There are many paths up the spiritual mountain. All roads lead to God.* The sentiments of mutual respect that underlie these mantras is well-meaning enough. But their simplistic gloss does exactly the opposite of what they intend. Rather than express a deep understanding of world religions, today's popular mantras convey flippancy and disrespect for them.

Take, for example, the mantra *All roads lead to God.* Christianity claims that only through Christ's atoning death on the cross can we be reconciled to God and delight in his presence for eternity. Islam disagrees with every aspect of that claim. In Islam, only if our good deeds outweigh our bad deeds and God has mercy on us will we enter into God's paradise. But

God himself is not there because he doesn't condescend to dwell among humans. In Hinduism, one is not trying to reach God, one is trying to become God. The Hindu scriptures teach that every person's soul—their *Atman*—is one with the divine, eternal absolute—the *Brahman*. Buddhism, on the other hand, was founded in rejection of the Hindu belief that we have a divine self. In classical Buddhism, there is no self at all and there is no divine being. Atman doesn't become Brahman because neither exists. There is simply the Void and our goal is to become extinguished into the Void. Confucianism is utterly uninterested in the afterlife at all. What matters is this life and the social structures in which we conduct ourselves. Not only are these roads all different, they also claim different destinations. How can all roads lead to God if not all the roads even claim to?

The Dignity of Difference

Fundamental differences between world religions is far more common than superficial similarities. To ignore our differences is to disrespect each other. In short, our differences make a difference. Affording to each other what I call "the dignity of difference" is key if we are to have genuine tolerance and a sincere journey to truth.

Though Buddhism shares some ideas with Hinduism, like reincarnation and karma, it sharply disagrees on other foundational ideas. Buddhism's "greatest contribution to the conversation among the great religions is its teaching that the thing we are most certain of—the self—is actually a figment of the imagination."[3] Fundamental to Hinduism, however, is the teaching that the self—the *Atman*—is one with the divine—the

Brahman. Unless you deny the self, you cannot be a Buddhist. Unless you affirm the divine self, you cannot be a Hindu.

Monotheistic faiths like Judaism, Christianity, and Islam claim that there is only one God and he is separate from and transcendent of his creation. Monistic Hinduism doesn't teach that there is only one God. Rather, it teaches that everything is God and God is all there is. Polytheistic Hinduism teaches that there are millions of gods, each being incarnations of the *Brahman.* Hinduism's beliefs are considered blasphemous in the monotheistic faiths, and the monotheistic faiths are considered misguided by Hinduism.

Human failings are viewed quite differently by the different faiths as well. In Islam, humans are born with an innate belief in God, called our *fitrah* (Qur'an 30:30). Our misdeeds come from ignorance or forgetfulness of God's commands. Christianity asserts that each of our transgressions is a symptom of the greater transgression of rebellion against God's original purpose for each of us. Unlike Islam, which claims we are born morally innocent, Christianity claims that we sin because we are sinful. In pantheistic religions like Buddhism and Hinduism, there is the cycle of karma. The bad deeds we commit in one life have consequences for us in the next life. Those negative consequences aren't punishments, they are exactly what they sound like: consequences. Bad circumstances in this life naturally result from misdeeds in a previous life, just like falling to the ground is the natural consequence of dropping a ball. In contrast to all these systems is Confucianism. With its emphasis on social structure, family duties, and the like, "Confucianism distinguishes itself from many other religions by its lack of interest in the divine."[4]

Recognizing and honestly wrestling with these diverse claims affords religious people the dignity of difference. If we don't acknowledge the fundamental differences, we end up disrespecting thousands of years of each religion's traditions and theological development. Personally, I take the claims of non-Christian religions too seriously to say that we all believe the same things. For the Muslim, it is blasphemous to believe that Jesus is the Son of God or that God is a triune being. In Christianity, it is heretical to deny those beliefs. How dare I tell a Muslim that she believes the same thing I do? To tell a Buddhist that his beliefs are basically the same as a Hindu's is to disrespect thousands of years of Buddhist thought. To claim that all roads lead to God isn't only illogical, it's disrespectful.

It isn't just the politically correct among us that have succumbed to the confusion. Some of us who would identify as religious believers claim (at least in some way) that all paths equally lead to God. During a panel discussion at a university I participated in with a Muslim imam and a Conservative Jewish rabbi, someone in the audience asked me to substantiate why I thought the Bible was the reliable Word of God. I was surprised to hear the imam agree with my defense of the Bible because the vast majority of Muslims believe that the Bible was once God's revelation, but became corrupted over time. And his surprising agreement wasn't just off-the-cuff. The imam actually expounded on why he thought the Bible was the Word of God.

After the event was over, a Christian student asked the imam how he could believe the Bible was the Word of God, yet disagree that it teaches that Jesus is the Son of God who died for our sins. As I was standing here, I couldn't help but hear his answer. The imam said that Jesus' claims in the Bible to be

God parallel similar statements Islam's Prophet Muhammad made about himself being eternal. But, because Islam forbids the idea that God could become human or that any human could be coeternal with God, Jesus' and Muhammad's statements must be understood esoterically. Neither Jesus nor Muhammad could have meant what they said. (As an aside, it's worth noting that the imam's theology comes from a mystical, unorthodox tradition within Islam called Sufism. No other orthodox Muslim would say that Muhammad even came close to deifying himself.)

Such thinking is confused for a few reasons. First, it's circular reasoning. The imam's reasoning went like this: Jesus isn't God. So when he claims to be God in the Bible, we have to interpret his claim esoterically because a literal interpretation would be blasphemous. Why? Because Jesus isn't God. The imam assumed the Islamic conclusion at the beginning of his argument. Second, in his attempt to show respect to Christianity, he ended up disrespecting it. For 2,000 years, Christians have understood Jesus' claims to divinity literally. The imam imposed his Islamic view of Jesus, that he was only a human prophet, onto the biblical account of Jesus' claims to be God (John 8:58), without taking thousands of years of Christian theology and biblical study seriously. He dismissed all of it in favor of his preferred interpretation.

This leads to the third level of confusion that goes beyond disrespecting religious difference and makes any religious claims unintelligible. Applying esoteric meanings to religious claims we don't prefer isn't *exegesis* (getting out of a religious text what it actually says) it's *eisegesis* (reading into the text what one wants it to say). Were we to apply that technique to all religions, they would become muddled and bland. When the imam said that Jesus couldn't be God, couldn't I esoterically interpret the imam as saying that he believes that Jesus really is God? In other words, I could use the same technique to ignore the imam's actual words to make them mean what I preferred. Or, I could esoterically interpret the imam as believing in pantheism (the belief that God is everything and that God is all there is) instead of Islam. When the imam claimed that there is only one God, what he esoterically meant was that there is only "one" God. It's interesting how an esoterically placed punctuation mark can misrepresent what someone actually meant.

Obviously, playing such word games is unhelpful, not just confused. There's even a sleight of hand at work here. *The Bible is the Word of God,* he claimed. But what he slipped in there was, *So long as it says what I want it to say.* I assume he wasn't being disingenuous. But the imam engaged in that kind of confused thinking because he wanted to (at least appear to) be ecumenical, religiously pluralistic, and multicultural.

This is fascinating, because so many in our culture employ the same kind of thinking and in the process end up abandoning the religious diversities they also champion. "You would think that champions of multiculturalism would warm to this fact, glorying in the diversity inside and across religious traditions," Prothero writes. But they are not warm to that fact. "Even among multiculturalists, the tendency is to pretend that the differences between, say, Christianity and Islam are more apparent than real, and that the differences inside religious traditions just don't warrant the fuss practitioners continue to make over them."[5] Prothero is mystified because diversity and tolerance seem to go hand in hand. Homogenization of religious beliefs doesn't lead to tolerance, it leads to confusion and ignorance. Mixing all religions together results in the colorless mess a child gets when she mixes all her colored paints together.

Tolerance only operates among differences, not sameness. No one has to tolerate ideas similar to their own. In fact, to speak of tolerance in such situations is meaningless. Tolerance implies not only differences but also stress and tension because of those differences. We measure the strength of metals by assessing how they tolerate stressors like vibration, heat, and cold. So too our tolerance levels are measured by the stresses of competing religious claims. We truly tolerate each other when our competing ideas are stressors. Different religious beliefs cause us to put our own beliefs to the test. That's true tolerance. And tolerance can lead to clarity.

The popular author and TV host Reza Aslan misunderstands this badly. Aslan has made quite a splash in the field of comparative religions, landing himself a miniseries on CNN called "Believer." Throughout the series, Aslan investigates different religions that are usually thought of as "extreme." He looks at the Aghori Hinduism, vodou in Haiti, and a doomsday cult, among others. Fascinatingly, Aslan is up-front that his agenda in making "Believer" is to smooth over the differences between religions.[6] He claims that the more he studies different religions, the more their similarities become evident.

Aslan's preference for all religions to be similar is the altar on which he has sacrificed not only a careful study of different religions but also reason itself. Aslan identifies as a Muslim. Interestingly, he converted from Islam to Christianity and then back again. Yet in the very first episode of "Believer," Aslan spends time with an Aghori Sadhus Hindu during which he actually eats charred human brains. The extremist Aghori believe nothing we ingest can defile us because everything is part of the divine. Wanting to show respect, Aslan ingests human flesh. It's fascinating that one of Islam's distinctives is its complex dietary laws. Yet Aslan was willing to eat something that would have made Muhammad apoplectic.

Aslan's confusion becomes evident when we compare his statements in two different publications promoting "Believer." In the *Los Angeles Times*, Aslan says, "There is no proof for the existence, or the nonexistence, of God and anyone who tells you otherwise is trying to convert you. Faith is a choice. But it's not an irrational choice. It is the result of one's empirical experience of the world, and of reality, and one's place in the world. You either believe that there is something beyond the material realm or you don't. And you can't be convinced, one way or the other."[7] In one statement, Aslan says both that there is no proof for or against God and that faith is a rational choice. How can belief be rational if there is no proof of it? Now I understand that he might be saying that there is no undeniable, conclusive proof. But judging from the rest of the context, Aslan appears to be saying that there isn't *any* proof. That's categorically false and, frankly, irrational.

In an opinion piece entitled "Why I am a Muslim," Aslan writes, "I know better than to take the truth claims of any religion (including my own) too seriously. But I also know this: Religion and faith are not the same thing. Faith is mysterious and ineffable. It is an emotional, not necessarily a rational, experience."[8] He says that faith is not irrational in one place but then says that it "is an emotional, not necessarily rational, experience" in another. What does he mean and how can these seeming contradictions be reconciled? Reading the broader context doesn't help:

> Let me be clear, I am Muslim not because I think Islam is "truer" than other religions (it isn't), but because Islam provides me with the "language" I feel most comfortable with in expressing my faith. It provides me with certain symbols and metaphors for thinking about God that I find useful in making sense of the universe and my place in it. But I know, just as the Buddha did, that while my personal well may be different and unique, the water I draw from it is the same water drawn from everyone else's wells. Indeed, having drunk from many wells in my spiritual journey, I consider it my mission in life to inform the world that, no matter the well, the water tastes just as sweet.[9]

Muhammad would disagree and so would Buddha. In fact, the Qur'an specifically says, "If anyone desires a religion other than Islam never will it be accepted of him; and in the Hereafter he will be in the ranks of those who have lost" (Qur'an 85:3). But, as Aslan admits, he doesn't "take the truth claims of any religion too seriously." So why should we take his show or views seriously?

I can't help but think of a discussion I had on this issue some time ago. I was speaking at a breakfast meeting about the differences between the major religions. Sitting in the front row was a man who was attentively listening and taking notes so quickly that I imagined smoke emanating from his paper. He approached me with some questions and comments when I was done speaking.

"Can I show you something?" he asked. When someone asks a speaker permission to "show you something," it's usually a signal that the ensuing conversation will not be brief. In the center of the page was a capital T. Surrounding it in a circle were lowercase t's, all with arrows pointing toward the capital T in the center.

"The capital T represents the objective total truth," he explained. "No human being knows all of the truth."

I agreed, of course. "Right. If we knew everything, we'd be God. But since I'm not God, I don't know everything and neither do you. So we're on the same page: neither of us is God."

I'm not sure he found that as funny as I did because he didn't skip a beat. "The lowercase t's represent all of us. We all have incomplete versions of the truth. Eventually, we'll become enlightened and have the gaps in our understanding filled in by the Absolute Truth."[10]

"Wait a second," I interjected. "Are you telling me that *everyone* has a version of the truth?"

"Yes!" he popped out. "Everyone."

"Really? Even people like Pol Pot, Mao Zedong, Adolph Hitler, or Joseph Stalin?"

The words that came next astonished me. "Well, I can't say that I prefer their versions of the truth. But, because all of our versions of the truth are incomplete, I can't say that I disagree with them either."

"Are you telling me that your worldview doesn't allow you to disagree with anyone else's?" I asked.

Excited that I was catching on, he exclaimed, "That's right! We can't really disagree with anyone."

"Sure you can," I said.

"No, I can't."

"You just did."

His animated hands dropped as he paused. He pressed on for a bit longer, but it became obvious that the Culture of Confusion—which elevates preferences over truth—had done its work in letting reason bleed to death under its knife. The man's preference was that everyone get along, that no one's convictions be challenged or scrutinized. He demoted truth and reason to elevate that preference. I'm convinced that this otherwise very intelligent man didn't know that he'd been doing that all along. He's certainly not alone, as so many of us sacrifice logic and truth on the altar of well-intentioned ecumenism. As Stephen Prothero says so well, "The ideal of religious tolerance has morphed into the straitjacket of religious agreement."[11]

Clarity about Jesus and the Gospel's Exclusivity

The straitjacket of religious agreement prevents us from getting our arms around the exclusive claims each faith tradition makes. Exclusivity has become something of a dirty word that's been leveled unfairly only at Christianity. But, as we'll see shortly, every religious system makes claims to have the exclusive truth. If we are to show respect to each faith, it's critical that we understand this.

Truth, by definition, is exclusive. As Ravi Zacharias has often said, every truth claim necessarily excludes its opposite as false. Even religious views that claim to be all-inclusive—like Baha'ism and some forms of Hinduism—are exclusive in that they claim that the exclusivists are wrong. If we confuse universal agreement with tolerance, we end up indicting every single religious (and even nonreligious) view as intolerant.

This is why Jesus' claim to be the sole means of salvation doesn't put him outside the realm of tolerance, but squarely within it. Jesus' claim is quite unequivocal. He says in John 14:6, "I am the way, and the truth, and the life. No one comes to the Father except through me." That statement isn't just an exclusive truth claim, it's uniquely exclusive. Where other religious founders claimed to *have* the way or to *have* the truth, Jesus claims to *be* the way and the truth.

Such a claim can't just sit out there. We would justifiably demand evidence to back it up, just as the religious leaders did when they heard Jesus' claims (John 2:18). Jesus' bodily resurrection ultimately vindicated his claim. Indeed, that signals another way in which Jesus' exclusive claims are unique. His audacious claim to *be* the way and truth is substantiated by objective proof. His physical body would either be dead or alive after the crucifixion. Preferences and opinions about it were (and still are) irrelevant. Peter's eyewitness of that resurrection emboldened him to preach the exclusivity of Christ to hostile crowds. "And there is salvation in no one else," Peter said about Jesus, "for there is no other name under heaven given among men by which we must be saved" (Acts 4:12).

I was a guest on a radio program a few years ago talking about Jesus' claims to exclusivity. A caller made the comment that Jesus' exclusivity claims are found only in the Gospel of John, the last gospel to be written and the one supposedly containing legendary embellishments. Aside from the fact that John's gospel doesn't contain such embellishments and is replete with eyewitness accounts of Jesus' life, it isn't true that only John records Jesus' exclusive claims. Take, for example, Matthew 21 and Luke 19, where we read of Jesus' entry into Jerusalem just before the Passover. As he entered the city riding on a donkey, his followers laid palm fronds before him and sang praises to him that were reserved only for God. The offended religious leaders demanded that Jesus silence the supposed blasphemy. Jesus responded with Psalm 8:2, which speaks of the praises God reserves *for himself*: "Out of the mouth of infants and nursing babies you have prepared praise" (Matthew 21:16). He drove the point home by saying, "I tell you, if these were silent, the very stones would cry out" (Luke 19:40).

This stands in stark contrast to the Qur'an, which says that Jesus was only a messenger and that the very idea of Jesus being God's Son is so "monstrous" that "the skies are ready to burst, the earth to split asunder, and the mountains to fall down in utter ruin" (Qur'an, Sura 19:89–92). In the Bible, if people stopped praising Jesus, nature would cry out in praise. In the Qur'an, when people do praise Jesus, nature cries out in protest. Christianity and Islam couldn't be more opposite on this important issue. Logic and respect dictate that we find out which, if either, is right.

Even if we recognize that all religions make exclusive claims, our Western culture tends to disfavor Christianity's exclusivism. A secular humanist friend complained of Christian arrogance in claiming to have the monopoly on spiritual truth while everyone else is consigned to hell. While that objection proceeds from a fundamental (and all-too-common) misunderstanding of the gospel, I think it can teach us something valuable. What he—and others—have perceived from some Christians is a triumphalist attitude about Jesus being the only way to God. While I unequivocally believe that he is, there are times when Christians affirm Christianity to be exclusively true because it's *their* religion.[12] It's one thing to affirm that the gospel is exclusive and true. It's quite another to be prideful about it. We may find it to be the case that non-Christians aren't so much protesting the fact that the gospel is exclusive, but the way Christians sometimes boast about it.

The gospel message is that we are all sinners, utterly undeserving of God's grace and mercy. We owe God a debt and are unable to pay it. Jesus paid that debt for us. Being fully God and fully human, Jesus was able to live a perfect life so that he had no sins of his own to pay for and could hang on that cross as our representative. The fact of our sin ought to quash any sense of pride in us. The fact that Jesus offered himself as payment for us ought to dismantle any prideful sense in us that the gospel is true because it is *ours*. Jesus didn't claim to be my truth, my way, and my life. He claimed to be *the* way, *the* truth, and *the* life. He isn't the exclusive Savior because he saved me. He's the exclusive Savior—the Lamb of God—who takes away the sins of the world. When both the Christian and the non-Christian see this, perhaps both will see the exclusive claims of Christ and his sacrifice for our sins not as the "secret password" that gains us entry into a special club, but as the humble actions of the Most High God, offered to each one of us, as lowly and wretched as we are.

Where the Truth Lies

Religious differences make a difference, but we have to recognize at least two elements common to all religious (and even nonreligious) systems of thought. Every view recognizes that the world is not as it should be. Something has gone wrong and is in need of fixing. According to Prothero, "What the world's religions share is not so much a finish line as a starting point. And where they begin is with this simple observation: something is wrong with the world."[13] This is an interesting point of common ground upon which we can discuss our differing solutions to the human condition. This commonality is related to another point of commonality among all worldviews—except the Christian worldview.

Decades ago, C. S. Lewis warned us that our love of the exotic and our "horror of the Same Old Thing" can entice us into embracing seemingly novel ideas that actually don't give us anything new.[14] In the West, especially amidst the Culture of Confusion, anything but the been-there, done-that Christian gospel seems to satisfy our spiritual hunger for novelty. To keep our menu as diverse as possible, many have embraced the notion that all worldviews—theistic, pantheistic, or nontheistic—are equally valid options. We've already seen that religions are only superficially similar (at best), but fundamentally divergent. Let's now plunge into a paradox to see the important ways in which every major worldview—except Christianity—is much the same.

There are, for example, surprising similarities between atheism and pantheism. Atheists deny God's existence (or at least claim to lack a belief in God). Yet many affirm that if there is an ultimate authority, humanity is it. When we throw off "the God delusion," we find that we have replaced God. In his well-known parable, Friedrich Nietzsche's Madman asks, "What festivals of atonement, what sacred games shall we have to invent now that we have replaced God?"[15] Now, compare that with pantheism—a worldview that nearly every atheist would claim is false. Pantheism (in its most influential iterations) basically teaches that "all is One, and all is divine." This means that there is only one spiritual reality and humanity is unified with it.

Do we see the paradoxical commonality? Atheism claims that humanity is the measure of all things and that we have the sole and ultimate authority for morality and destiny because there is no God. Likewise, pantheism teaches us we are the measure of existence because God is all there is. Strange, is it not, that one worldview rejects any divine existence while the other says that there is only a divine existence, and yet they both glorify humanity as the ultimate?

Secular humanism, Islam, and pantheism share a more profound commonality that sharply differentiates them from the Christian gospel. Undergirding those worldviews is the belief that every person can earn, and therefore deserves, an ultimate reward. For the secular humanist, humanity is the master of the universe, coming up with the ethical rules by which to live. And through our own magnificence we will educate ourselves out of the mess we're in (and that we created). For pantheists (depending on the type), we are "gods in embryo," all-powerful "thetans," or "one with the universe." Buddha and his followers ascribed to "history's most dangerous idea," namely that we can solve humanity's problem without relying on God. As such, we create reality and we—through our meditations, self-audits, good deeds, or right thinking—can enlighten ourselves out of the mess we've created. Similarly, "Confucians have always had a faith, bordering on fanaticism, in the ability of human beings to improve and even perfect themselves."[16] And in Islam, though we always need God's mercy to get us past our misdeeds, we can earn God's mercy when our good works outweigh our bad deeds (Qur'an 7:8–9). It's fascinating that worldviews that are so different can be so much of the "Same Old Thing" when it comes to human entitlement to utopia.

In contradistinction to all these views is the Christian gospel. Where atheism tells us that we are the measure of all things, the gospel tells us that God is the standard by which we are measured. Where pantheism tells us that our problem is that we have forgotten that we are God, the gospel tells us that our problem is that we wanted to *be* God rather than commune with God. Where Islam tells us that we can earn God's forgiveness, the gospel tells us that such a view is self-contradictory and only Jesus' payment for our sins solves the contradiction.

The gospel tells us we are sinners. Human history corroborates that claim. The gospel tells us we are the problem and so, quite logically, cannot be the solution, nor can we be trusted to follow the rules. The fact that nearly every other worldview seeks to make humanity the achiever of salvation or utopia suggests that they are human-made worldviews. We do have a tendency for self-justification and aggrandizement, after all.

But the gospel tells us that our self-aggrandizement is the very thing that gets us into trouble. We need someone who is not us to save us from ourselves. Jesus is that someone. While this idea that we need a savior doesn't prove the gospel is true, it does provide us with a clue that humans didn't make it up. If we had, we would have put ourselves as the gospel's centerpiece. But Jesus is the centerpiece, the way, the truth, and the life. He is all three and offers them to us freely so that we don't need to forge them ourselves. That good news is about as far away from the "same old thing" as one can get.

Observing differences and similarities among worldviews helps us to gain clarity on the answers to life's most important questions. Our common recognition that the world is in need of fixing serves as the platform from which we can see which of the different pools that offer solutions are worth jumping into. Some pools will be too shallow. Others will be entirely empty. Only one has an ocean's depth.

Christ and Convergence

Allow me to close this chapter on differences by pointing to the unexpected way aspirations and hopes from other worldviews converge in Jesus.

It has always fascinated me that people from widely different worldviews find Jesus so attractive and claim him as their own. In Islam, Jesus is a sinless, virgin-born prophet of God (the Qur'an has more verses about Jesus than any other figure, including Muhammad). Many Hindus, like Gandhi, admire Jesus as an enlightened teacher. Some even believe that Jesus is an incarnation of the beloved god Vishnu. I know of Buddhists who consider Jesus to be a *bodhisattva*, or incarnation of Buddha, much like the Dalai Lama. Even atheists will acknowledge that Jesus was "a pretty good guy." Stephen Prothero sums up Jesus' impact: "There is no disputing the influence Jesus has had on world history. The Library of Congress in Washington, DC, holds more books about Jesus (roughly seventeen thousand) than about any other historical figure—twice as many as the runner-up, Shakespeare. Worldwide, there are an estimated 187,000 books about Jesus in five hundred differ-ent languages. Jesus even has a country named after him: the Central American nation of El Salvador ('The Savior')."[17]

Everyone wants a piece of Jesus. He is a champion, a teacher, an exemplar, or a prophet. Why? Because the person of Jesus, revealed to us in the Gospels, is compelling. Kids rushed to play with him in the sunlit day, and religious schol-ars secretly met with him in the moonlit night. Women found wholeness in him and thieves found forgiveness. Sinners were convicted by his words, but also redeemed by his actions. Jesus is the convergence of everything we wish were true about our worldviews and about ourselves.

Our nearly universal affinity for Jesus is the bright side of this convergence. But our human desire to strip Jesus of his cross is the darker side. As everyone tries to make Jesus their world-view's mascot, they must either deny the crucifixion (as in Islam) or deny its meaning (as in atheism, pantheism, and even theo-logically liberal strands of Christendom). Jesus can't be what we want him to be if he died to pay for our sins. And our preference above all others is that we don't need to be saved by someone else. We can save ourselves. We are autonomous. So the cross must either be shelved away or reduced to decorative jewelry.

Jesus' disciple, Peter, tried that too. In Matthew 16:15, Jesus asks his disciples, "Who do you say that I am?" Always ready with a response, Peter correctly answers that Jesus is the Christ. But when Jesus explains that the Christ came to die as a substi-tution for sinners, Peter rebukes him because he wants Jesus to vanquish the Roman overlords. Jesus is nothing less than blunt with his friend: "Get behind me, Satan! You are a hindrance to me. For you are not setting your mind on the things of God, but on the things of man" (v. 23). Peter knew the truth about who Jesus was, but he had to get past what he preferred Jesus to be. Eventually, Peter saw past his preferences and embraced Jesus' death and resurrection. Indeed, he was martyred so we could know who Jesus really is.

Our Culture of Confusion—which tries to make all religions equal and rob Christ of his cross—is strikingly similar to Peter. We admire Jesus so much, yet we tailor him to fit our preferred worldviews. In so doing, we are very much like another of Jesus' disciples, Judas, who betrayed Jesus with a kiss.

Jesus beckons us to lay down our preferences and consider who he really is. By doing so, he offers us the beauty of real choice. Drawing on his Christian roots, James Madison wrote in *A Memorial and Remonstrance*, "Whilst we assert for ourselves a freedom to embrace, to profess and to observe the Religion which we believe to be of divine origin, we cannot deny an equal freedom to those whose minds have not yet yielded to the evidence which has convinced us."[18] Jesus gave us verifiable evidence that he is God incarnate who came to this earth to give his life in payment for our transgressions. That evidence gives us the freedom to choose to believe in him, based not on chaotic emotional preferences, but on information.

Only an informed choice is a meaningful choice. Imagine a game in which you're given three doors to choose from. One door will give you $1 million, another will give you nothing, and another will cost you $1 million. Now, if you aren't given any information to help you pick the right door, would you have a meaningful choice or is your choice up to chance? Sure, you could freely choose any door, but your choice wouldn't be meaningfully free. If you were provided evidence that allowed you to make an educated decision, your choice becomes infused with meaning. Your humanness would be involved in the choice. This is the gospel's distinctive. One's choice to accept or reject it is based on propositions that we can know are either true or false. In other belief systems, one's choice is based largely on preferences and personal experience and sometimes cultural coercion. By making the test for his claims falsifiable, Jesus respects our rational faculties. Thus, he attracts the empiricist within us. He also speaks to us in a way that inspires our hearts, so he is also attractive to the artists in our souls.

The major religions of the world agree that there is something wrong with the world and with us. The Qur'an says that if God were to judge humanity according to what it deserves, the whole world would be destroyed (Sura 35:45), and yet it says that there is no divine intervention to take that evil away from us, because "no bearer of burdens can bear the burden of another" (Qur'an Sura 6:164; 17:15). Hinduism and Buddhism tell us that we are left to deal with the bad karma we've accreted. And yet the Hindu poet Tukaram poetically beseeched the god Narayana to take his burden from him:

> Thy name will carry me over the sea of this world,
> Thou dost run to help the distressed,
> Now run to me, Narayana, to me, poor and wretched as
>   I am.
> Consider neither my merit nor my faults.
> Tukaram implores thy mercy.

The "bearer of burdens" that the Muslim is looking for is found in Jesus. His sinlessness freed him from bearing any sinful burdens of his own, making him able to bear ours. The one who the pantheist looks for, who considers neither our merit nor faults to give us mercy, isn't Narayana or any other god. It's Jesus, who clothes us with his merit. This is the beauty of the cross Isaac Watts so beautifully wrote about:

> When I survey the wondrous Cross
> On which the Prince of Glory died
> My richest gain I count but loss
> And pour contempt on all my pride
> Forbid it, Lord, that I should boast
> Save in the death of Christ my God
> All the vain things that charm me most
> I sacrifice them to his blood
>
> See from his head, his hands, his feet
> Sorrow and love flow mingled down
> Did e'er such love and sorrow meet
> Or thorns compose so rich a crown?

God grants us the dignity of embracing or rejecting Christ as our Savior. But lest we be confused and think that gospel is an exclusive club, the most famous passage of the Bible gives us clarity. In John 3:16 we read, "For God so loved *the world*"—that's everyone—"that he gave his one and only Son, that *whoever* believes in him"—that's anyone—"should not perish but have eternal life" (NIV). The Christian message is that there is an exclusive way to get to God. And that one way cost God more than it will ever cost us. But the invitation to accept it includes us all.

CHAPTER 9

The Son through Fog: Clarity's Hope

Hope. It's the feeling or desire that things will work out for the best. We use it to express sentiments both mundane—*I hope the coffee shop is still open because I could really use a latte*—and profound—*I hope that my marriage doesn't fail.* In either case—mundane or profound—we hope for things to work out because we are uncertain that they will. In other words, we often hope because we are unsure. We further weaken our grip on hope by celebrating confusion as virtuous while decrying clarity as sinful. Our grasp can be strengthened if we reorient our wistful gaze from the foggy unsure to the clear.

The controversial issues of our day act like fault lines that erode the bedrock of clarity. Controversy is made up of two Latin words—*contra*, meaning against, and versus or *vertere*, meaning to turn. Controversy arises, quite literally, when we turn against something or someone. We think of controversies most often as a public debate over opposing views. And indeed controversy has flourished in our day when autonomy is the ultimate goal. When our individual autonomies collide, the inevitable result will be to turn against each other. One compound word—autonomy—leads to another—controversy.

But controversy's deepest fissures aren't public. They're private. They roil within each of us. One may champion unrestrained freedom, yet subconsciously recognize that true freedom must be bound by truth. A person may want to define her own sexual and gender identity, only to find that fulfillment remains elusive. We try to limit our worldview to what science can measure, but then stare at the horizon wondering if there's more to life than this mortal coil. Our preferences have not given us the sure footing of clarity's dry land, only the wobbling buoyancy of confusion's river.

These internal controversies—not the public ones—make the gospel's simple clarity appealing yet difficult to embrace. And the gospel really is simple. It is the good news that you and I are sinners in need of a savior and Jesus is that Savior. Because he is perfect, you don't have to be. He will perfect you. Because of what God has done in the past, we can have faith in what he will do in our futures. Secular hope is uncertain. Biblical hope is sure.

Can something so simple be all-encompassing? Is it too good to be true? How can one idea—indeed one person, Jesus—clarify our culture's confusion and bring us the clarity we need? The world is too big for any one worldview, isn't it?

Indeed, to say that the gospel is simple yet all-encompassing seems contradictory, but it isn't. In fact, it's our fragmentation of life that's too small to handle this world. We see no overarching, simple idea that connects all our fragmented views. We've so obsessed over the freedom to do what we want that we've neglected the freedom to do what we should. To wrap our minds around what it means to be human, we've focused narrowly on brain chemistry, thereby reducing ourselves to freedomless chemical machines. This in turn leads us to contradictorily conclude that with regard to sexual and gender identity, we're "born that way" but should be allowed to explore as many sexual or gender expressions as we want. We give lip service to respecting all religions only to turn against a particular religion if it doesn't line up with our irreligious autonomy. Of course, life is complicated. And yes, we need nuanced answers to life's questions. A stained glass window is complex too. But the outer frame that holds its intricate pieces together is usually a simple square or circle. We must embrace this paradox to find clarity: the comprehensive answers to life's complicated questions emanate from one straightforward worldview. Chesterton brilliantly summarized the ineffability of this paradox. "A man is not really convinced of a philosophic theory when he finds that something proves it," Chesterton writes. "He is only really convinced when he finds that everything proves it. And the more converging reasons he finds pointing to this conviction, the more bewildered he is if asked suddenly to sum them up."[1]

We can become convinced that one worldview, a simple idea, offers hope because it corrals all of life's complexities. Chesterton observed that one can be convinced of something when he or she finds that everything proves it. But the inverse is also true. We can be convinced of something when we find that it proves everything else. The gospel says we are not automatons slavishly responding to external stimuli but are beings with physical bodies, nonmaterial minds, and free will. This substantiates humanism. The gospel tells us that our sexual and gender identities are not our ultimate identities. This satisfies our desire for intimacy. The gospel embraces scientific inquiry as a means to investigate the natural world because that investigation satisfies our God-given sense of wonder. The gospel allows us the dignity of differing on matters of faith while claiming to be the sole spiritual truth. This addresses our desire for coherence. Life's innumerable complexities are marshaled under one clarity: we are made in God's image; the cross and empty tomb demonstrate how valuable that image is. In short, everything "proves" the gospel and the gospel "proves" everything. With such clarity, our fingers wrap tighter around a sure hope for a better future. This may seem an audacious claim in light of Christendom's historical black eyes. While Christianity's abuse has brought hate's darkness, it's pure form has brought hope's light. The atheist philosopher and former Italian senator Marcello Pera agrees:

> If we live as Christians, we will be wiser and more aware of the dangers we face. We will not separate morality from truth. We will not confuse moral autonomy with any free choice. We will not treat individuals, whether the unborn or the dying, as things. We will not allow all desires to be transformed into rights. We will not confine reason within the boundaries of science. Nor will we feel alone in a society of strangers or oppressed by the state that appropriates us because we no longer know how to guide ourselves.[2]

Yes, worldviews other than Christianity have contributed positively to society. But Marcello Pera isn't saying that Christianity just contributes positively to our hope. He's saying that it is the foundation for our hope.

From Russia with Hope

I was at an event during which a secular humanist physician challenged the idea that the gospel uniquely brings hope. The good of humanity, he protested, is all that we need for us to find hope for the future. We don't need God or the gospel, just each other. He went so far as to claim that atheists are often better than religious people in light of how many have died at religious hands. When it was pointed out to him that multiple millions more have died under atheistic regimes like Stalin's Russia and Mao's China, he refused to accept that atheism had anything to do with it. "That's communism," he said. "None of that was done in the name of atheism." To brush off Stalin's and Mao's murderous atrocities as communism's fault ignores the role that Stalin's and Mao's atheism played in establishing their communist regimes. Karl Marx, the godfather of communism, saw belief in God as the opiate of the people that kept humanity numb to the schemes of the powerful. That's why a colleague of mine had to smuggle Bibles under the Iron Curtain in the 1980s. When he came to a Soviet-controlled border, the guards would ask him three questions: *Are you bringing guns? Are you bringing drugs? Are you bringing Bibles?* Communist regimes are not incidentally atheistic. They are foundationally atheistic. Atheism is as woven into communism as theism is into Christianity.

Yet amid long breadlines, an anemic economy, and the brooding scowl of government dominance, hope endured in the Soviet Union. The wellspring for its endurance was the gospel message itself. A husband and wife from Belarus taught me that at a recent backyard party. As our children played together in the nearby pool, the husband asked me for my kids' names. When I told him that my youngest child is named Nadia, he was surprised to learn that Nadia is a common name to Arabs as well as Eastern Europeans. The Russian version, he told me, is *Nadiajda*, which means "hope." He went on to say that the three most popular girls' names—even during the Soviet Union—were *Vera*, which means "faith," *Nadiajda*, which means "hope," and *Lubov*, which means "love."

It was my turn to be surprised. In the purposefully atheist Soviet Union, the people expressed their hearts' cry through the names of their children—faith, hope, and love. How poetic that God inspired the apostle Paul to string those three words together as the pearls of life's God-given meaning. "And now these three remain: faith, hope and love" (1 Corinthians 13:13, NIV). Like millions who lived under Communist regimes, Paul was no stranger to experiencing material want and suffering religious oppression. Yet faith, hope, and love bolstered his endurance. An entire generation of Russians who endured Stalin and the hardships of failed communism literally bear the names faith, hope, and love—*Vera*, *Nadiajda*, and *Lubov*.

The Son shines through the fog, giving us the light to find our own hope in the post-truth Culture of Confusion. Like the Soviet Union, the Culture of Confusion will not last forever. Clarity will eventually return. But it won't happen just by the passage of time. Clarity will return most fully when we see the gospel for what it is and see Jesus for who he is. I've seen clarity return in individual lives right before my eyes. During a three-day speaking trip, an intelligent young man engaged with me on some thorny issues. He came to every event during those three days, each time asking poignant questions. His final question summed up the pathos behind all of his previous ones. "Why would God create human beings he knew would sin and then send them to hell for eternity? Doesn't that seem inconsistent with a belief that God is all good?"

His question was a moral one, which meant that he would have had to assume the existence of objective moral values for his question to make sense. Fascinatingly, he denied that objective moral values exist: "I'm not assuming anything. I'm asking you—who does believe in objective morality—to be consistent."

"*Should* I be consistent?" I asked.

"Of course," he said.

"Why?" I asked. "If there aren't objective moral values, then I can either lie in my answer to you or I can blurt out meaningless sounds. The answer would be just as meaningful (or meaningless) either way, and I wouldn't have done anything morally wrong. But you just said that I *should* be consistent. If I *should*, then you actually do believe I have a moral obligation to tell the truth. Who's being inconsistent here?"

He saw where I was going and had a response. "No, I'm not saying we should be consistent because it's morally good. I'm saying we should be consistent because truth helps us to survive and flourish as a species."

But that isn't the case within an evolutionary worldview. Truth is irrelevant to survivability and flourishing. We could just as easily survive or flourish by believing something false. The young man said he was an atheist. But studies show that religious people tend to live longer and happier lives than the irreligious.[3] So I asked him, "If there is no God, should we still believe in him because doing so is good for the species?" He was hard pressed to say yes because he was caught in a conundrum. He had a love of logic and a strong moral compass (despite denying it). He could escape the conundrum only by seeing that morality is an inescapable part of a world filled with meaning and coherence.

The answer to his question provides a key to unlocking hope's door. *Why would God create beings he knew would die rejecting him and be consigned to hell?* For the skeptic and Christian alike, that question is not merely intellectual. It's personal because it involves human suffering. One way to approach the answer is to see that we aren't meant to be puppets dancing on God's marionettes. We are created to have fulfilling, everlasting intimacy with God. That relationship entails the freedom to embrace or reject God. That intended purpose—true relationship—turns the question on its head. For the Christian, the question really isn't, *Why would God create people knowing that their rejection might hurt them?* The question is: *Why would God create free people knowing that their rejection would hurt him?*

Let's unpack that a bit. First, God doesn't need us to have relationship. As a triune being, God exists with three distinct personalities—Father, Son, and Holy Spirit. He has always had perfect relationship. This means that he creates us not so that he can have relationship, but so that we can. Second, relationships happen only when at least two parties exercise their wills to make it happen. We are imperfect creatures, which means that we will express our wills imperfectly. In other words, we will have an imperfect relationship with God that could include rejecting him. Thus, creation was always going to include the risk that some of us would reject God.

Third, we often think of that rejection's consequences as one-sided: *we* reject God and *we* suffer for it. But that ignores a fundamental truth: our rejection affects God as well. To God, we are immeasurably valuable whether we embrace or reject him. "Precious in the sight of the LORD is the death of his saints," the Bible says in Psalm 116:15. And God declares, "I have no pleasure in the death of the wicked" (Ezekiel 33:11). Relationships where at least one party is imperfect always entail vulnerability. When we enter into a marriage or even just a friendship, there is always the possibility that one of us will reject the other, leaving at least one person wounded. We try to guard against such wounds by choosing whom to let into our lives. Sometimes we do so wisely, sometimes unwisely. But we still have the opportunity to shield ourselves from rejection's sting.

God doesn't pick whom he loves, which means that the pain of rejection is not probable, it's inevitable. We object to the way God created the world out of concern for the pain we *might* feel. We forget about the pain that God *will* feel. If we go to heaven, the pain of our lives will be wiped away. But God, no matter how many are in heaven with him, will eternally remember—and perhaps eternally grieve—the loss of those who chose not to spend eternity with him. His pain over our rejection is as eternal as he is.

Why spend so much time on this one question here? Because the answer clarifies God's selfless character. And that selfless character crystalizes our hope.

From Freedom to Truth— From Truth to Clarity

As we close, let's return to Jesus' statements in John 8. "You will know the truth, and the truth will set you free" (v. 32). There can be no freedom without truth; there can be only chaotic autonomy. Jesus goes one step further and identifies himself with the truth: "If the Son sets you free, you will be free indeed" (v. 36). The Son is the truth that leads to our freedom. Ravi Zacharias and I presented those ideas during an open forum at Yale. An insightful student asked us a question, the answer to which will help us tie all of the ideas we've wrestled with in this book together. "While I can understand fairly intuitively the connection between truth and freedom . . . I struggle a little bit with the connection between Jesus and truth and Jesus as the necessary viewpoint to truth as opposed to say science or some other religion. You both hinted at the resurrection as a catalyzing moment for the validity of the Christian religion and the validity of Jesus as truth. I'm just wondering if you could expound a little bit on that?"

The answer is that Jesus' historically verifiable resurrection vindicates his claim that his death pays the debt we've incurred for our sins. Jesus—as God the Son incarnate—paid an immeasurable price for us. If something's value is determined by its price, then Jesus' payment demonstrates that each one of us—you and me—are immeasurably valuable. Jesus' payment provides us with freedom from sin, and his resurrection provides us with life so we can be free to be what we were intended to be.

Two thousand years later, our post-truth Culture of Confusion has elevated personal preferences over truth. The musical group Crash Parallel captures the spiraling hopelessness that comes from filling our lives with things that are neither true nor personal:

Well sleepless nights and endless days
And Miniskirts and serving trays.
Waking up from rain delays,
And selling sex for pocket change.
And living off the alcohol
With no one but a cab to call.
And lost inside a bathroom stall,
This carbon copy life withdrawal.
And driving cars we can't afford,
Just making sure we're never bored.
Living off our own accord
Between coffee grinds and corner stores.
And limousines and cigarettes,
And chasing dreams with fishing nets
And long weekends without regrets,
Well no one here is taking bets.
And I need someone to believe in.
Yes someone to fill this space with grace
Someone to look into my eyes and touch my face,
To make me feel alive today.
Someone to make me strong
Someone to make me belong
Someone to make it alright
Someone to make me feel alive.[4]

We don't need some*thing* to make us alive. We need some*one*.

In Christ truth and personal feelings converge. Both are important. In our zeal for autonomy, we've fallen into confusion by elevating personal feelings above truth. But we have to be careful not to succumb to the equally confused idea that cold hard facts alone will liberate us. Truth has to be personal if it is to touch our minds and hearts. There are facts that are important for certain pursuits, but they are limited in their importance. Water boils at sea level at 100 degrees centigrade. That's helpful to know if one is a chemist, and it might come in handy if one is cooking pasta. But I doubt that water's boiling point will help us fall back asleep when life's anxieties stalk our minds late at night. While truth isn't determined by personal preferences or need, it becomes relevant when it fulfills our legitimate needs. As Clifford Williams so astutely puts it: "Need without reason is blind, but reason without need is sterile."[5]

In Jesus Christ, we have both the truth who satisfies our quest and the personality who satisfies our need for connection. He is the truth our minds seek and the person our hearts embrace. He validates facts and personal preferences without sacrificing either. His words expose the fact of our sin. The fact of his sacrifice demonstrates his unbounded love for us. And the fact of his resurrection provides us with the joy of knowing our desires can be fulfilled. There they are: joy and knowledge, feeling and fact, coupled together. Putting it all together is how we go about saving truth.

A post-truth culture that elevates feelings over facts gives us only half the picture. And in being half right, it's all wrong. It offers us only the flowing river, not the steady land. Two thousand years ago, Jesus claimed to be the truth that sets us free. In the ensuing centuries, we've elevated personal preferences over truth, thinking that we can be fulfilled of our own accord. Yet we've filled our lives with material trappings and experiences that are neither true nor personal.

Jesus is the river and the land, the fount of living water and the rock of our salvation. He secures humanity's freedom to be what we were intended to be: sacred beings in relationship with the divine. When we realize that, confusion dissipates like fog and clarity remains. *What is truth?* we may ask in a world that elevates personal preference over truth. The answer is Jesus— the truth who is personal. He is the Saving Truth.

ACKNOWLEDGMENTS

No man is an island, the Bible says. We need each other and I've needed the help of so many in completing this book. Randy Pistor painstakingly reviewed each chapter and helped me with research. Brian Wassom, himself an accomplished writer, provided valuable insights that helped me simplify difficult concepts. Mickey Badalamenti, a lifelong friend, engaged in long conversations with me on the ideas and insights that eventually made their way into this book. Without their help, this work wouldn't have been possible.

I'm grateful for the assistance of my friend and colleague, Stuart McAllister. His deep understanding and breadth of reading on cultural trends made it important to get his confirmations of where I was headed in this book. Nick Peters provided some helpful research for which I'm very thankful. I'm also indebted to Sam Allberry for taking the time to review the chapter on sexuality and gender identity. His experience, his compassion, and his understanding on these topics were simply invaluable. My executive assistant, Tara Brody, spent long hours trying to decipher the cuneiform that passes for my handwriting, making edits well into the night so that the manuscript could be done on time and with quality. I am grateful for the editorial insights from Madison Trammel with Zondervan. This book is undoubtedly better because of his keen sense of how to tighten wording.

Most importantly, I wish to thank my wife, Nicole, and my children. Nicole read each chapter with my intended audiences in mind. But she and our children did so much more than that. They extended me the grace to work long hours researching, writing, and editing. Because they believe in me and my calling to engage others in tough discussions—and because they love others as they love themselves—they have sacrificed much. Their sacrifice has awed and humbled me.

NOTES

Chapter 1: The Blossoming of the Culture of Confusion

1. Ravi Zacharias makes this observation and analysis in his article "The Death of Truth and a Postmortem," December 20, 2016. http://rzim.org/global-blog/the-death-of-truth-and-a-postmortem/.

2. I remember hearing this analogy in a line from the 1995 film *Things to Do in Denver When You're Dead*, and it stuck.

3. To be sure, those who think that a post-truth mindset is a good thing don't think of themselves as having a post-truth mindset. Very few of us would actually admit valuing opinions and preferences over truth, and even fewer of us would admit that we willingly lie to serve a higher agenda. But just because we don't admit to something (or even realize that we believe it) doesn't mean that we don't agree with it. Our actions, not our admissions, are what expose our real beliefs.

4. Kathleen Higgins, "Post-Truth: A Guide for the Perplexed," *Nature* Magazine, November 28, 2016, reprinted online at *Scientific American*, December 5, 2016, https://www.scientificamerican.com/article/post-truth-a-guide-for-the-perplexed/#.

5. Ibid.

6. Adam Hoffman, "Biomedical Science Studies Are Shockingly Hard to Reproduce," January 4, 2016, Smithsonian.com. http://www.smithsonianmag.com/science-nature/biomedical-science-studies-are-shockingly-hard-reproduce-180957708/.

7. Brian Handwerk, "Scientists Replicated 100 Psychology Studies,

and Fewer than Half Got the Same Results," August 27, 2015, Smithsonian.com. http://www.smithsonianmag.com/science -nature/scientists-replicated-100-psychology-studies-and-fewer -half-got-same-results-180956426/.

8. Ioannidis JPA (2005) "Why Most Published Research Findings Are False." PLoS Med 2(8): e124. doi:10.1371/journal. pmed.0020124.

9. Hoffman, "Biomedical Science Studies Are Shockingly Hard to Reproduce."

10. Ibid.

11. Stephen Marche, "The Left Has a Post-Truth Problem, Too. It's Called Comedy," *Los Angeles Times*, January 6, 2017. http:// www.latimes.com/opinion/op-ed/la-oe-marche-left-fake-news -problem-comedy-20170106-story.html.

12. Ibid.

13. *The Passion of the Christ*, directed by Mel Gibson (Icon Entertainment International, 2014).

14. C. S. Lewis, *Mere Christianity* (San Francisco: HarperSanFrancisco, 2001), 32.

15. Genesis, "Land of Confusion," by Mike Rutherford, Tony Banks, and Phil Collins. Atlantic US, 1986.

16. G. K. Chesterton, *Orthodoxy* (New York: Doubleday, 2001), 33–34.

17. Blaise Pascal, *Pensées*, vol. 33.

Chapter 2: Confusion and the Church: Seductions of a Post-Truth Mindset

1. See *Fowler v. Thomas Nelson Publ'ing*, 2009 U.S. Dist. Lexis 17245 (E.D. Mich. 2009).

2. My initial response was that it sometimes bugs me that people, especially Christians, are a bit too eager to pick at flaws they see in their local churches' pastors. Any critique should be

measured with due respect for what the church is doing right. The fact is, being a pastor is a much tougher job than it used to be.

3. David Kinnaman and Gabe Lyons, *Good Faith: Being a Christian When Society Thinks You're Irrelevant and Extreme* (Grand Rapids: Baker, 2016), 27.

4. Ibid.

5. Ibid.

6. Kinnaman and Lyons, *Good Faith*, 59, quoting Dallas Willard, *Knowing Christ Today* (New York: HarperOne, 2009), 199–200.

7. Marie Chapian, *Of Whom the World Was Not Worthy* (Minneapolis: Bethany House, 1978), 122.

8. Bradley R. E. Wright, *Christians Are Hate-Filled Hypocrites . . . and Other Lies You've Been Told* (Bloomington, MN: Bethany House, 2010).

9. For guidance on ethical uses of social media, see Brian Wassom, *What Would Jesus Post?* (Nashville: Westbow, 2013).

10. Ed Stetzer, "Christians, Repent (Yes, Repent) of Spreading Conspiracy Theories and Fake News — It's Bearing False Witness," *Christianity Today Online*, May 31, 2017, www .christianitytoday.com/edstetzer/2017/may/christians-repent -conspiracy-theory-fake-news.html.

11. Mary Rich and Joel Rich, "We're Seth Rich's Parents: Stop Politicizing Our Son's Murder," Washington Post, May 23, 2017, www.washingtonpost.com/opinions/were-seth-richs -parents-stop-politicizing-our-sons-murder/2017/05/23/ 164cf4dc-3fee-11e7–9869-bac8b446820a_story.html?utm _term=.21f23f46aec9.

12. Adam Clarke, *Memoirs of the Wesley Family* (London: J. Kershaw, 1823), 270 (emphasis mine).

13. C. S. Lewis, *Mere Christianity*, 118.

14. Paul Lee Tan, *Encyclopedia of 7700 Illustrations: Signs of the Times* (Garland, TX: Bible Communications, 1996).

15. David Bentley Hart, *quoting* Julian, Epistle 22, *Atheist Delusions: The Christian Revolution and Its Fashionable Enemies* (New Haven, CT: Yale University Press, 2009), 45.

16. Matthew Parris, "As an Atheist, I Truly Believe Africa Needs God," December 27, 2008, *The Times Online*, www.thetimes .co.uk/article/as-an-atheist-i-truly-believe-africa-needs-god -3xj9bm80h8m (emphasis mine).

17. Chapian, *Of Whom the World Was Not Worthy*, 123.

Chapter 3: Confusion's Consequences—Getting Freedom Wrong

1. Jens Zimmermann, *Incarnational Humanism: A Philosophy of Culture for the Church in the World (Strategic Initiatives in Evangelical Theology)* (Downers Grove, IL: InterVarsity Press, 2012), 37.

2. An account and analysis of this incident can be found in Connor Friedersdorf, "The New Intolerance of Student Activism," *The Atlantic*, November 9, 2015, https://www.theatlantic .com/politics/archive/2015/11/the-new-intolcrancc-of-student -activism-at-yale/414810/.

3. Eugene Volokh, "Administrator's defending student free speech is apparently reason to remove the administrator, according to some Yale students," *The Washington Post*, November 7, 2015, https://www.washingtonpost.com/news/volokh-conspiracy/ wp/2015/11/07/administrators-defending-student-free-speech -apparently-reason-for-dismissal-according-to-some-yale -students/?utm_term=.1956371055de.

4. Interestingly, on August 29, 2017, a group of Ivy League professors, including Nicholas Christakis, issued a powerfully worded encouragement to students to think for themselves, even if it means being labeled offensive or a crank. See "Some

Thoughts and Advice for Our Students and All Students," James Madison Program, August 29, 2017, https://jmp .princeton.edu/announcements/some-thoughts-and-advice -our-students-and-all-students.

5. Thomas Sowell, quoted in Beverly A. Potter and Mark J. Estren, *Question Authority to Think for Yourself* (Berkeley, CA: Ronin, 2012), 86.

6. Facebook has since streamlined the choices to male, female, or "custom."

7. See chapter 6.

8. Jackie Willis, "Miley Cyrus Sees Herself as a 'Genderless Spirit,'" *ET Online*, June 23, 2017, www.etonline.com/news/ 220229_miley_cyrus_sees_herself_as_a_genderless_spirit _i_m_just_a_spirit_soul/.

9. Julie Scelfo, "A University Recognizes a Third Gender: Neutral," *New York Times*, February 3, 2015, www.nytimes.com/ 2015/ 02/ 08/ education/ edlife/ a-university-recognizes-a-third-gender -neutral.html?_r = 0& module = ArrowsNav& contentCollection = Education% 20Life& action = keypress& region = FixedLeft& pgtype = article.

10. Tom Flynn, "Secular Humanism Defined," July 7, 2012, www .secularhumanism.org/index.php?section=main&page=sh _defined4.

11. Jeremy Rifkin, *Algeny: A New Word—A New World* (New York: Viking, 1983), 244.

12. Alexander Pope, "Essay on Man," in *Essays on Man and Other Poems*, 3rd ed. (New York: Dover, 1994), 48 (public domain).

13. Peter Singer, "Why It's Irrational to Risk Women's Lives for the Sake of the Unborn," *The Scotsman*, August 15, 2012, www.scotsman.com/thescotsman/opinion/comment/analysis -why-it-s-irrational-to-risk-womens-lives-for-the-sake-of-the -unborn-1-2467196.

14. Ibid.

15. Alberto Giubilini and Francesca Minerva, "After-Birth Abortion: Why Should the Baby Live?" *Journal of Medical Ethics* (March 2, 2012), 2.
16. David Bentley Hart, *Atheist Delusions: The Christian Resolution and Its Fashionable Enemies* (New Haven, CT: Yale University Press, 2009), 23.
17. This, of course, ignores the psychological impact that such an action would have on the parents after murdering their child.
18. Yuval Noah Harari, *Sapiens: A Brief History of Humankind* (New York: HarperCollins, 2015), 415–16.
19. California Senate Bill No. 219. 1439.51(a)(5). http://leginfo .legislature.ca.gov/faces/billCompareClient.xhtml?bill _id=201720180SB219.
20. See Michael Shermer, "The Unfortunate Fallout of Campus Postmodernism—The Roots of the Current Campus Madness," *Scientific American*, September 1, 2017, https:// www.scientificamerican.com/article/the-unfortunate-fallout -of-campus-postmodernism/.

Chapter 4: Clarity about Freedom

1. Os Guinness, *A Free People's Suicide: Sustainable Freedom and the American Future* (Downers Grove, IL: InterVarsity Press, 2012), 57–58.
2. Ibid., 61, citing Isaiah Berlin, *Four Essays on Liberty* (New York: Oxford University Press, 1969), 118 (emphasis mine).
3. Ibid. (emphasis mine).
4. Guinness, *A Free People's Suicide*, 63.
5. Ibid., 65.
6. David Foster Wallace, "Everybody Worships," commencement address at Kenyon College, 2005, reprinted at http://www .mbird.com/2008/09/more-david-foster-wallace-quotes/ (September 20, 2008).
7. Os Guinness points out the irony of the fact that it is in the

societies where negative freedom is all the rage, millions are in addiction-recovery programs. *A Free People's Suicide,* 151–52.

8. I'm grateful to Brian Wassom for referring me to Adams' statement in this letter.

9. Guinness, *A Free People's Suicide,* 20.

10. G. K. Chesterton, Orthodoxy (New York: Doubleday, 2001), 36–37.

11. Kai Nielsen, "Why Should I Be Moral?" *American Philosophical Quarterly* 21 (1984): 90.

12. Richard Dawkins, *River Out of Eden: A Darwinian View of Life* (New York: Basic Books, 1995), 133.

13. Raymond Tallis, *Aping Mankind: Neuromania, Darwinitis and the Misrepresentation of Humanity* (Durham, UK: Acumen, 2011); Thomas Nagel, *Mind & Cosmos—Why the Materialist Neo-Darwinian Conception of Nature Is Almost Certainly False* (Oxford: Oxford University Press, 2012).

14. For a summary of some of these perspectives, including Sam Harris's views, see Stephen Cave, "There's No Such Thing as Free Will—But We're Better Off Believing in It Anyway," *The Atlantic,* June 2016, https://www.theatlantic.com/magazine/archive/2016/06/theres-no-such-thing-as-free-will/480750/. See also Sam Harris, *Freewill* (New York: Free Press, 2012).

15. Ibid.

16. Matthew 15:19.

17. "A Secular Humanist Declaration," Council for Secular Humanism, issued 1980, accessed August 16, 2017, https://www.secularhumanism.org/index.php/11.

18. Gary R. Habermas and Michael R. Licona, *The Case for the Resurrection of Jesus* (Grand Rapids: Kregel, 2004); Michael R. Licona, *The Resurrection of Jesus: A New Historiographical Approach* (Downers Grove, IL: InterVarsity Press, 2010).

19. Abdu Murray and John Loftus, "Did Jesus Rise from the Dead?" https://www.youtube.com/watch?v=66E-OykI9UY.

20. Mary Poplin, *Is Reality Secular? Testing the Assumptions of*

Four Global Worldviews (Downers Grove, IL: InterVarsity Press, 2014), 124–25.

Chapter 5: Clarity about Human Dignity

1. "Golden Rule, Iconic Norman Rockwell Mosaic, Rededicated at UN Headquarters," U.N. News Centre, February 5, 2014, www.un.org/apps/news/story.asp?NewsID=47089#. WbAS5a2ZORs.
2. Dominique Janicaud, *On the Human Condition, Thinking in Action* (New York: Routledge, 2005), 1.
3. *Planned Parenthood of Southeastern Pa. v. Casey*, 505 U.S. 833, 851 (1992).
4. *Obergefell v. Hodges*, 135 S. Ct. 2584 (2015).
5. Paul Kurtz, "Humanist Manifesto 2000," *Free Inquiry*, Fall 1999, available at www.secularhumanism.org/index.php section=main&page=manifesto.
6. Humanist Manifestos I and II, 17 (emphasis added).
7. European Union, Preamble to "Treaty Establishing a Constitution for Europe," 9, October 29, 2014, accessed August 30, 2017, http://news.bbc.co.uk/2/shared/bsp/hi/pdfs/oi_01_05_constitution.pdf (emphasis added).
8. Abdu H. Murray, *Grand Central Question—Answering the Critical Concerns of the Major Worldviews* (Downers Grove, IL: InterVarsity Press, 2014), 45–116.
9. Daniel C. Dennett, *Consciousness Explained* (New York: Back Bay Books, 1991), 33.
10. Lawrence Krauss, quoted by Richard Panek, "Out There," *New York Times*, March 11, 2007, www.nytimes.com/2007/03/11/magazine/11dark.t.html?_r=1.
11. Peter Atkins, *The Second Law*, 2nd ed. (New York: Scientific American Books, 1994), 200.
12. Michael Ruse, "God Is Dead. Long Live Morality," *The*

Guardian, March 15, 2010, accessed November 2, 2017, www.theguardian.com/commentisfree/belief/2010/mar/15/morality-evolution-philosophy.

13. Daniel C. Dennett, *Darwin's Dangerous Idea: Evolution and the Meaning of Life* (New York: Touchstone, 1995), 63.

14. John Gray, *Straw Dogs* (London: Granta, 2003), 48.

15. "The Personal Philosophy of Richard Posner," *The Big Think*, April 23, 2012, www.youtube.com/watch?v=jYa5y8IkUMk.

16. Paul Kalinithi, *When Breath Becomes Air* (New York: Random House, 2016), 49.

17. Peter Singer, "Sanctity of Life or Quality of Life?" *Pediatrics*, 72, no. 1 (July 1983), 128–29.

18. See Harris's comments in Stephen Cave's "There's No Such Thing as Free Will."

19. Tallis, *Aping Mankind*, passim.

20. See J. P. Moreland's considerable body of work on the subject, including J. P. Moreland, *The Soul: How We Know It's Real and Why It Matters* (Chicago: Moody, 2014); J. P. Moreland, *Consciousness and the Existence of God: A Theistic Argument* (New York: Routledge, 2008); J. P. Moreland and William Lane Craig, *Philosophical Foundations for a Christian Worldview* (Downers Grove, IL: InterVarsity, 2003), 228–46. The well-known atheist philosopher A. J. Ayer experienced a near death experience that he could not explain in natural terms. A. J. Ayer, "What I Saw When I Was Dead: Intimations of Immortality," *National Review*, October 14, 1988, 39–40. See also Karl R. Popper and John C. Eccles, *The Self and Its Brain* (New York: Springer-Verlag, 1977), 558, where they note that Nobel Prize–winning physiologist Sir Charles Sherrington declared five days before his death: "For me now, the only reality is the human soul."

21. Tallis, *Aping Mankind*, 83.

22. Ibid., 108–109.

23. Ibid., 10.

24. "Phil 103—Liz Harmon on Abortion," http://www.youtube
.com/watch?v=r55QnQjryzl&feature=youtube.

25. Tallis, *Aping Mankind*, 348.

26. John Gray, "Stephen Pinker's Delusions of Peace," ABC
Network, www.ABC.net.au/articles/ 2013/01/20/ 3672846.htm.

27. C. E. M. Joad, *The Recovery of Belief* (London: Faber and
Faber, 1952), 81–82.

28. C. S. Lewis, *God in the Dock* in *The Timeless Writings of C. S.
Lewis* (Grand Rapids: Eerdmans, 2003), 311.

29. Singer, "Sanctity of Life or Quality of Life?"

30. C. S. Lewis, *The Weight of Glory* (New York: HarperOne,
2001).

Chapter 6: Clarity about Sexuality, Gender, and Identity

1. Thomas Bracken, *Not Understood and Other Poems*
(Wellington, NZ: Richard Brown, 1905), 7–8 (public domain).

2. International Gay and Lesbian Human Rights Commission
[IGLHRC], Institutional Memoir of the 2005 Institute for
Trans and Intersex Activist Training (2005): 7–8, https://iglhrc
.org/sites/default/files/367–1.pdf.

3. See Kevin DeYoung, *What Does the Bible Really Teach about
Homosexuality?* (Wheaton, IL: Crossway, 2015), for a discussion
of how biblical passages have been interpreted to justify same-
sex behavior and how to properly interpret those same passages.

4. Sam Allberry, *Is God Anti-Gay? And Other Questions About
Homosexuality, the Bible, and Same-Sex Attraction* (Epsom:
Surrey, UK: Good Book, 2013), 25.

5. Michael W. Hannon, "Against Heterosexuality," *First Things*,
March 2014, https://www.firstthings.com/article/2014/03/
against-heterosexuality.

6. Jenell Williams Paris, *The End of Sexual Identity: Why Sex*

Is Too Important to Define Who We Are (Downers Grove, IL: InterVarsity Press, 2011), 40.

7. Ibid., 128.

8. Ibid., 9.

9. Richard Dawkins, "Growing Up in the Universe" (Royal Institution Christmas lectures, London, 1991), cited by John Lennox, "Challenges from Science," in *Beyond Opinion*, ed. Ravi Zacharias (Nashville: Thomas Nelson, 2007), 116.

10. "Gay Prince Is Cut Off from His Fortune for 'Dishonouring His Family,'" http://www.telegraph.co.uk/news/worldnews/asia/india/1522558/Gay-prince-is-cut-off-from-fortune-for-dishonouring-his-family.html.

11. There have been various and quite solid responses to these attempts to reinterpret the Bible as same-sex sexuality affirming. I recommend Sam Allberry's short book, *Is God Anti-Gay?*; Rosaria Champagne Butterfield, *The Secret Thoughts of an Unlikely Convert: An English Professor's Journey into Christian Faith* (Pittsburgh: Crown and Covenant, 2012); Butterfield, *Openness Unhindered: Further Thoughts of an Unlikely Convert on Sexual Identity and Union with Christ* (Pittsburgh: Crown and Covenant, 2015); and Kevin DeYoung, *What Does the Bible Really Teach about Homosexuality?* (Wheaton, IL: Crossway, 2015).

12. "Studies Find Escalation (and Habituation) in Porn Users," at yourbrainonporn.com, https://www.yourbrainonporn.com/studies-find-escalation-porn-users, accessed November 27, 2017.

13. This isn't to say that sexual activity between a married man and woman must be limited to procreation. But there is no denying that heterosexual intercourse is inextricably tied to human life. And life is precious. It is sacred. It is beautiful. And because of that, sexuality is worth the protections with which God has surrounded this beautifully intimate act.

14. Allberry, *Is God Anti-Gay?*, 25.

15. Mark A. Yarhouse, *Understanding Gender Dysphoria—Navigating Transgender Issues in a Changing Culture* (Downers Grove, Ill.: IVP Academic, 2015), 9.

16. For more comprehensive lists with definitions, see Yarhouse, *Understanding Gender Dysphoria*, particularly chapter 1. In Andrew Walker, *God and the Transgender Debate: What Does the Bible Actually Say about Gender Identity?* (Purcelville, VA: Good Book, 2017), Walker includes a helpful appendix of definitions.

17. Yarhouse, *Understanding Gender Dysphoria*, 20.

18. Ibid., 92.

19. Ibid., 58.

20. Walker, *God and the Transgender Debate*, 68.

21. Cecile Dhejne, Paul Lichenstein, Marcus Bowman, Anna L. V. Johansson, Niklas Langstrom, and Mikael Landon, "Long-Term Follow Up of a Transsexual Person Undergoing Sex Reassignment Surgery: Cohort Study in Sweden," *PLoS one*, 2011; b(2): e16885, www.ncbiinlm.nih.gov/pmc/articles/PMC3043071. For a list of other studies with similar findings, see Yarhouse, *Understanding Gender Dysphoria*, 119, n.bb; see also Richard P. Fitzgibbons, "Transsexual Attractions and Sex Reassignment Surgery: Risks and Potential Risks," *Linacre Quarterly*, 82.4 (2015): 337–50, PMC.Web.28Sept.2017.

22. Matt Moore, "I Begged God to Make Me Straight and He Never Answered," http://faithit.com/begged-god-make-straight-never-answered-matt-moore/ (emphasis added).

23. Ibid.

24. Melinda Selmys, personal communication with Mark Yarhouse, April 13, 2014, quoted in Yarhouse, *Understanding Gender Dysphoria*, 59–60.

25. Emily Brontë, "The Prisoner," originally published in 1864. Accessed at *The Literature Network*, www.online-literature.com/bronte/1356/.

Chapter 7: Clarity about Science and Faith

1. Richard Dawkins, *The God Delusion* (London: Bantam, 2006), 5. This quote is Dawkins's amalgamation of the Microsoft Word definition of delusion and a pithy quote from Robert Pirsig's *Zen and the Art of Motorcycle Maintenance*.

2. Edward J. Larson and Larry Witham, "Scientists Are Still Keeping the Faith," *Nature* 386 (1997): 435–36.

3. Isaac Newton, *Opticks: Or A Treatise of the Reflections, Refractions, Inflections and Colours of Light*, 4th ed., London, 1730 (Mineola, NY: Dover, 1952), 369–70.

4. David Bentley Hart, *Atheist Delusions: The Christian Revolution and Its Fashionable Enemies* (New Haven, CT: Yale University Press, 2009), 61, 64–65.

5. Michael Ruse, "Is Darwinism a Religion?" The Huffington Post Blog, July 21, 2011, http://www.huffingtonpost.com/michaelruse/is-darwinism-a-religion_b_904828.html.

6. David Berlinski, *The Devil's Delusion: Atheism and Its Scientific Pretensions*, 2nd ed. (New York: Basic Books, 2009), 10.

7. David Hume, *An Enquiry Concerning Human Understanding* (London: 1748; Minneapolis: Filiquarian, 2007), 147, 149.

8. Alvin Plantinga, *Where the Conflict Really Lies: Science, Realism, and Naturalism* (Oxford: Oxford University Press, 2011).

9. Thomas Nagel, *Mind & Cosmos: Why the Materialist Neo-Darwinian Conception of Nature Is Almost Certainly False* (Oxford: Oxford University Press, 2012), 27–28.

10. David Bentley Hart, *The Experience of God: Being, Consciousness, Bliss* (New Haven, CT: Yale University Press, 2014), 70.

11. Murray, *Grand Central Question*, 97–102; 107–113.

12. Charles Darwin, *The Descent of Man* (Seattle: Madison Park, 2011), 87.

13. Richard Weikart, *From Darwin to Hitler: Evolutionary Ethics, Eugenics, and Racism in Germany* (New York: Palgrave Macmillan, 2004), 232–33.

14. See Hugh Ross, "Thank God for Perfect Solar Eclipses," July 10, 2017, http://www.reasons.org/explore/blogs/todays-new -reason-to-believe/read/todays-new-reason-to-believe/2017/07/10/ thank-god-for-perfect-solar-eclipses.

15. Ibid.

16. See Hugh Ross, *Improbable Planet: How the Earth Became Humanity's Home* (Grand Rapids: Baker, 2016), 41–42.

17. For more on this argument, see J. P. Moreland and William Lane Craig, *Philosophical Foundations for a Christian Worldview* (Downers Grove, IL: InterVarsity Press, 2003), 465–67.

18. Paul Davies, *Superforce: The Search for a Grand Unified Theory of Nature* (New York: Simon and Schuster, 1984), 235–36.

19. Despite this incisive statement, Davies is not, to my knowledge, a theist. Rather he ascribes to something similar to panpsychism—the belief that the universe itself has a mind and sort of fashions itself. For a number of reasons, I think this view falls short of explaining how the universe got here. For example, a panpsychic material universe still needs to be explained by an immaterial noncontingent being. Nevertheless, the point remains that a world-class physicist like Davies acknowledges that it looks like choices were made in the fashioning of the universe.

20. Ryan Whitwam, "Simulating 1 Second of Human Brain Activity Takes 82,944 Processors," *Extreme Tech*, August 4, 2013, www.extremetech.com/extreme/16305-simulating-1 -second-of-human-brain-activity-takes-82,944-processors.

21. Dr. Rana describes biomimetics and bioinspiration in more

detail in chapter 8 of Josh Shoemaker and Gary Braness, *God and the World of Insects* (Silverton, OR: Lampion, 2017).

22. Francis Crick, *Life Itself* (New York: Simon and Schuster, 1981), 88.

23. Francis Crick, *What Mad Pursuit—A Personal View of Scientific Discovery* (New York: Basic Books, 1990), 138.

24. F. W. Boreham, *The Luggage of Life*, (Grand Rapids: Kregel, 1995), 78–85.

Chapter 8: Clarity about Religious Pluralism

1. See, for example, James W. Sire, *The Universe Next Door: A Basic Worldview Catalog*, 5th ed. (Downers Grove, IL: IVP Academic, 2009); Winfried Corduan, *Neighboring Faiths: A Christian Introduction to World Religions* (Downers Grove, IL: IVP Academic, 2012); Stephen Prothero, *God Is Not One: The Eight Rival Religions That Run the World—and Why Their Differences Matter* (New York: HarperCollins, 2010); and Ravi K. Zacharias, *Jesus Among Other Gods—The Absolute Claims of the Christian Message* (Nashville: W Group, 2002).

2. Prothero, *God Is Not One*, 1.

3. Ibid., 179.

4. Ibid., *God Is Not One*, 106.

5. Ibid., 12.

6. Reza Aslan, interview by Seth Myers, *Late Night with Seth Myers*, March 1, 2017, accessed April 22, 2017, https://www.youtube.com/watch?v=vjr_xM1DXLw.

7. Stephen Battaglio, "In CNN's 'Believer,' Reza Aslan to Aim for a Window on World Religions," *LA Times*, http://www.latimes.com/entertainment/tv/la-et-st-reza-aslan-believer-cnn-20150321-story.html.

8. Reza Aslan, "Why I am a Muslim," political op-ed, CNN,

February 26, 2017, accessed April 22, 2017, http://www.cnn
.com/2017/02/26/opinions/believer-personal-faith-essay-reza
-aslan/index.html.

9. Ibid.

10. He was mixing Christian language with Mahayana Buddhism,
which teaches that there are conventional truths (lowercase t)
and an Absolute Truth (uppercase T). From the perspective of
Absolute Truth, everything is empty and there are no distinctions
between any of us, regardless of how different our views may be.
For a lengthier explanation, see Prothero, *God Is Not One*, 195.

11. Ibid., 4.

12. Christians don't corner the market on arrogance, not even
close. Anyone who has engaged in theological discussions,
especially on social media, knows this.

13. Prothero, *God Is Not One*, 11.

14. C. S. Lewis, *The Complete C. S. Lewis Signature Classics—The
Screwtape Letters #25* (San Francisco: HarperSanFrancisco,
2002), 175–76.

15. Friedrich Nietzsche, *Modern History Sourcebook: Nietzsche:
Parable of the Madman*, http://www.fordham.edu/halsall/mod/
nietzsche-madman.asp.

16. Prothero, *God Is Not One*, 110.

17. Ibid., 70–71.

18. "Memorial and Remonstrance against Religious Assessments,
[ca. 20 June] 1785," *Founders Online*, National Archives, http://
founders.archives.gov/documents/Madison/01-08-02-0163.

Chapter 9: The Son through Fog: Clarity's Hope

1. G. K. Chesterton, *Orthodoxy* (New York: Doubleday, 2001), 84.

2. Marcello Pera, *Why We Should Call Ourselves Christians: The
Religious Roots of Free Societies* (New York: Encounter, 2011),
160–61.

3. Frank Newport, Dan Watters, and Sangeeta Agrawal, "In U.S., Very Religious Have Higher Wellbeing Across All Faiths" (February 16, 2012), www.gallop.com/poll/152732/Religious -Higher-Wellbeing-Across-Faiths.aspx.
4. Crash Parallel, "Rain Delays," in *World We Know,* Sony BMG Canada, 2008. Used with permission.
5. Clifford Williams, *Existential Reasons for Belief in God—A Defense of Desires and Emotion for Faith* (Downers Grove, IL: IVP Academic, 2011), 12.